CONSTITUTIONAL
HISTORY OF THE
AMERICAN REVOLUTION

ABRIDGED EDITION

CONSTITUTIONAL HISTORY OF THE AMERICAN REVOLUTION

ABRIDGED EDITION

John Phillip Reid

THE UNIVERSITY OF WISCONSIN PRESS

The University of Wisconsin Press
114 North Murray Street
Madison, Wisconsin 53715

3 Henrietta Street
London WC2E 8LU, England

1   3   5   4   2

Printed in the United States of America

Library of Congress Cataloging-in-Publication Data
Reid, John Phillip.
Constitutional history of the American Revolution
John Phillip Reid.—Abridged ed.
170 p.   cm.
Includes bibliographical references (p. 129) and index.
ISBN 0-299-14660-X (cl.)   ISBN 0-299-14664-2 (pbk.)
1. United States—Constitutional history. 2. United States—
Politics and government—1775–1783. I. Title.
KF4749.R45   1995
342.73'029—dc20
[347.30229]   94-39045

9857350

ER

For

William E. Nelson

and his colleagues at the
New York University School of Law Legal History Colloquium

ROBERT J. KACZOROWSKI
JOHN H. BAKER
WILLIAM P. LAPIANA
HENDRIK HARTOG
RONALD BROWN
LAWRENCE FLEISCHER
MICHAEL LES BENEDICT
JAMES C. OLDHAM
LARRY KRAMER
PETER CHARLES HOFFER
JUDITH T. SCHOLL
ELIZABETH B. WILSHIRE
WILLIAM MICHAEL TREANOR
RACHEL VORSPAN

SARAH B. GORDON
MARTIN S. FLAHERTY
EBEN MOGLEN
HOWARD VENABLE
RICHARD B. BERNSTEIN
CHRISTOPHER EISGRUBER
HAROLD M. HYMAN
BARBARA WILCIE KERN
DONALD G. NIEMAN
NORMAN CANTOR
EDWARD A. PURCELL, JR.
GERALD GIANNATTASIO
LOUISE ANTELL HALPER
WALTER J. WALSH

CONTENTS

HISTORIOGRAPHICAL PREFACE

"The dispute between Great-Britain and her colonies is now reduced to a single point," a "Citizen of Philadelphia" told his fellow American colonists in 1774. That question was, "*Whether the Parliament shall give laws to America.*"[1] He was speaking to future generations of Americans as well, telling them that the civil war that would soon begin on the green at Lexington, Massachusetts, would be precipitated by a constitutional dispute over customary restraints on power, the meaning of those restraints, and how they were defined. The overriding constitutional concern of the English-speaking people of the eighteenth century was with the exercise of power. Power was feared in the first British Empire: the power of "factions," power that was arbitrary, corrupt, unchecked, and unconstitutional. Above all, political theorists, constitutionalists, and just plain citizens were apprehensive of the arbitrariness of "will and pleasure," whether it was the caprice of a single ruler, an oligarchy, or that of the fickle, unpredictable democratic majority, sometimes called the "mob."

Fear of arbitrary power was one side of the constitutional debate that preceded the American Revolution. The other side was American adherence to English constitutional principles. Colonial whigs would fight the Revolution not only against the British Parliament but on behalf of the British constitution. That constitution, as they interpreted it, defended customary, prescriptive, contractarian rights against the onslaught of government's assertions of arbitrary power. The constitution to which Americans appealed did not only restrain power on behalf of the rights of the "people." More significantly, it restrained parliamentary command by enforcing the rule of law. That was the principle that would divide the Americans from the British. For American whigs, constitutional law meant that legislative command was subject to the rule of law. For the British, command of the legislature was law. By 1776, the American revolutionary dispute had come to center on whether those conflicting definitions of law could be reconciled.

The theoretical framework erected by historians to explain the American Revolution has always been fluid. Just when the contours of hypothesis settle on a model of general consensus, new historiographical concepts introduce radical shifts of emphasis leaving past patterns of interpretation to atrophy, while the mainstream of historical writing bursts its old banks to wind a totally new course or return to an abandoned river-bed.

As a general rule, one school of thought usually dominates the field. Writers of the generations that took part in the Revolution or personally knew its participants largely described it as a struggle about constitutional government.[2] Later, through much of the nineteenth century, the "whig" or "nationalist" school reigned supreme. The nationalists oversimplified the Revolution by employing the standard stereotype of a patriotic struggle between liberty and tyranny as a common denominator explaining all the complex issues and events of those gravid times.[3]

As historical scholarship became more scientifically critical, the complaint arose that nationalist writers had made the Revolution as much a conservative as a popular movement.[4] Adapting techniques and perspectives of the emerging disciplines of economics and social science, two new schools of revolutionary history came to the front. One was the institutional historians, led by Charles M. Andrews, Herbert L. Osgood, Robert Livingston Schuyler, and Lawrence H. Gipson. These scholars emphasized the role of institutions rather than the values of individuals. A school within this school were the imperialists. The dominant institution of the late eighteenth century, they taught, was the British Empire. The Empire was controlled by the British ministry in Whitehall. What Whitehall decreed was the law, and that fact settled all disputes about constitutionality. The one exception to this approach among the institutional imperialists was Charles Howard McIlwain. His great work on the constitutional interpretation of the American Revolution, however, needs revision as he relied too much on an argument based on the analogy between Ireland and the colonies which was not legally accurate, and on a theory of legal positivism that belonged more to the twentieth than to the eighteenth century.[5]

The progressive socio-economic historians rivaled the institutionalists.

Also utilizing the new tools of economics and social science, they created a radically different approach, one as cynical as it was objective. Postulating at least two related historical theories—the theory of twin revolutions (one revolution against Great Britain to obtain home rule and the second between Americans to determine who should rule at home)[6] and the theory that the American Revolution was essentially a two-phase class struggle (a democratic revolution by the masses followed by a conservative counter-revolution)[7]—the socio-economic determinists described the Revolution as the outcome of economic and social forces rather than "the result of the actions of wicked men." The Revolution was now a "clash between rival systems of mercantilism and the differentiation of the colonists from citizens of the Mother Country through the influence of an agricultural frontier."[8]

Neither of the socio-economic schools reigned for long. During the 1950s and early 1960s a new group of historians undercut the foundation on which the dual-revolution or class-struggle theory of the American Revolution had been based. Using the tools forged by the socio-economic school, but without its smug faith in historical iconoclasm, they mustered evidence proving that the previously accepted picture of colonial society was false:[9] that the government of prerevolutionary Massachusetts was not controlled by a merchant aristocracy;[10] that with land-owning and voting privileges universally distributed in Massachusetts there "was undoubtedly more economic democracy for the common man then than there is now";[11] that what "has been proven about the franchise in early Massachusetts—that it was open for practically the entire free adult male population—can be proved to a lesser or greater extent for all the colonies";[12] and that since the class structure of the revolutionary period was a "ramp" on which "[t]he progression from class to class on the scale of wealth . . . was a continuous and even flow," it is wrong to think of those years as a time of class antagonisms or class struggle.[13] For these historians—the "neowhig" or "consensus" school— "the Revolution was *not* revolutionary; its purpose, indeed, was to preserve the *status quo*";[14] to preserve, that is, "liberties already enjoyed,"[15] "the large measure of liberty and prosperity that was already part of their way of life."[16] Surprisingly, they, too, tended to ignore the constitutional dimension, perhaps because the discovery that the American Revolution was a defense of the status quo contained such implications of constitutionalism that they dismissed the topic as so obvious it did not need discussion.

The consensus school dominated for no more than a generation, its place taken by a group of ideological historians who did not read words as they had been read in the eighteenth century. They also did not assume that the ideas debated by both sides explained the theories of the revolutionaries or the imperialists, and, certainly, they did not believe that ideas determined motivations. "Instead of studying individuals and the ideas they articulated,"

Joyce Appleby has pointed out, "the new ideological historians highlighted the ways that societies construct 'reality' through shared discourses. Where whig history had assumed that human nature endowed men with an independent capacity to size up reality, ideology—a concept that refers to the structuring of thinking—encloses human consciousness within a social skein of organized reasoning."[17] Jack P. Greene added: "What has been until recently almost completely ignored and what, it now appears, is vastly more important [than the formal concepts of political thought and the external forms of institutional development], is that elusive and shadowy cluster of assumptions, traditions, conventions, values, modes of expression, and habits of thought and belief that underlay these visible elements."[18]

Had these scholars paid closer attention to eighteenth-century rather than twentieth-century concepts, they might have noticed that the discourse that shaped the "reality" of American whigs was framed in constitutional terms, and that the assumptions, traditions, conventions, and values were all to a large extent constitutionally based. A culture of constitutionalism pervaded that epoch more than in any previous times and certainly more than during the two centuries since.[19]

The ideological historians were not enticed. They endorsed the notion of "the autonomy of ideas"—that "ideas operate, as it were, over the heads of the participants, taking them in directions no one could have foreseen."[20] Even though taking ideas seriously, they reconstructed eighteenth-century ideology as a comprehensive system of thought in which constitutionalism was but one contributing element of the contemporary world view. They therefore discounted the degree to which people, leaders as well as educated commoners, were motivated by constitutional anxieties. Several considerations led them away from constitutional law.

1. They dismissed American arguments as nonconstitutional borrowings from the polemical literature of the British political opposition, when, in fact, both American whigs and the opposition in London were within the mainstream of constitutional tradition. What the ideological school did not consider was that the colonists and most people in Great Britain put their trust in the English constitution of customary, prescriptive rights, the constitution discussed in this book, and not, as the ideological school assumed, the British constitution of sovereign command, the constitution in force in Britain today.[21]

2. They tended to equate consitutionalism with the fungible and evanescent nature of politics rather than the principled application of law. It is this perspective as well as their training as historians that has led members of the ideological school to treat as ahistorical the repetition in English history from century to century of similar constitutional arguments. The constitutional case made by American whigs, for example, was "remarkably similar"

to that of the parliamentarians who had opposed Charles I's assertion of arbitrary power. "The ideas of the Americans seem, in fact, to form what can only be called a revolutionary syndrome," one member of the ideological school has complained. "It is not that this syndrome of ideas was simply transmitted from one generation or from one people to another. It was rather perhaps that similar, though hardly identical, social situations called forth within the limitations of inherited and available conceptions similar modes of expressions."[22] With that statement we see the ideological historians tiptoeing up to the constitutional explanation, and then stepping back rather than risk being drawn into consideration of anything so mundane as the learning of lawyers. By eschewing the constitutional, they missed a key fact of English politics—the persistence of constitutionalism over time. The colonists of the 1760s were opposing claims by Parliament to arbitrary power. From the constitutional perspective, they were the same claims that Parliament in the 1640s had opposed when made by Charles I. The Americans of the 1770s and the English of the 1640s used similar modes of expression because they were appealing to the same seventeenth-century constitution of customary, prescriptive rights, not to the nineteenth-century constitution of sovereign command.

3. Ideological historians also did not give sufficient credit to how constitutional law often determined the course of political events in the eighteenth century. "The common law," a founder of the school has written, "did not in itself determine the kinds of conclusions men would draw in the crisis of the time. . . . The law was no science of what to do next."[23] Maybe not, but constitutional law was a guide of when and how to take a stand against the government's exercise of unprecedented power, of what parliamentary actions should be opposed and on what grounds.

4. A few ideological historians have too readily dismissed much of the American whig constitutional argumentation as "the paranoiac obsession with a diabolical Crown conspiracy." "[T]he Americans' peculiar conception of reality," it has been assumed, "convinced them that tyranny was afoot" and that there was a conspiracy among leaders of the British government to deprive them of their liberties.[24] There is much evidence that can be cited showing that the colonists believed in a conspiracy, but there also are reasons why the conspiracy explanation should be taken with grains of salt. One is constitutional law. A maxim of that law was that "the king can do no wrong." At the time of the American Revolution that meant that "whatever may be amiss in the conduct of public affairs is not chargeable personally on the king; nor is he, but his ministers, accountable for it to the people."[25] As a result of that rule, a rhetoric existed in English politics of speaking of the crown indirectly, of saying that it was not the king who was at fault, but some unnamed conspirator behind the throne. It was a method of political po-

lemics apparently hiding from twentieth-century scholars precisely what
was being said, but not fooling the people of that day. It was a method of
discussing public affairs familiar to the eighteenth century, a way of saying
things that met the expectations of most readers. We may glimpse the
technique by considering how the leading expounder of the conspiracy
theory interpreted arguments Americans were making just before passage
of the Stamp Act. "For the colonists did not then [1764] consider the King
or even Parliament guilty of deliberate malice toward America," he writes.
"The evil lay not with the King but with certain advisers, twisted plotters
pursuing factious aims and corrupting public policy. The King and his Privy
Council had been misinformed. . . . "[26]

5. The ideological school, by attempting to occupy a "shadowy middle
ground between constitutional history and cultural history,"[27] was also led
away from constitutionalism by the attractive nuisance of a bright, shiny
ideological theory labelled "republicanism." The scholars of the 1980s concluded that "the colonists [had] reasoned within a classical republic logic
that linked the British imperial reforms of the 1760s and 1770s to Renaissance teachings about the state."[28] The basic element of republicanism was
civic virtue, sometimes defined "as willingness to abide by the laws of a just
state even when prudent self-interest might recommend disobedience."[29]
Again, they failed to recognize the extent to which republicanism and eighteenth-century constitutionalism resonate off one another. One result is that
republicanism, as it has been interpreted by students explaining the American Revolution, has become a discourse that does "not bear the same
meaning for everyone,"[30] a model "so complex . . . as to be almost unintel-
ligible."[31] Such was also true for the eighteenth century. James Madison,
Thomas Jefferson, Alexander Hamilton, and John Adams all had different
definitions of republicanism. As lawyers they also had their political notions
anchored in contemporary law and constitutionalism, helping them to avoid
what has been described as the "[c]urrent disillusionment with republicanism," which has led some members of the ideological school to an intellectual dead end, to the belief that "we lack a methodology or theoretical vocabulary capable of handling the paradoxical nature of political discourse,
which is sometimes highly determinate and sometimes mysteriously elusive,
and that we do not currently possess an analytical construct to link the
diverse political languages spoken in early America with its complex socio-
logical realities."[32]

The construct would have been less elusive had the ideological historians
paid closer attention to eighteenth-century discourse than to their own. The
discourse of both American whigs and British imperialists was a discourse of
rights: discussion of constitutional rights dominated the revolutionary literature, not a "reality" informed by classical republican ideas lifted from an-

cient and renaissance texts. The argument of this book is not that law alone explains the coming of the American Revolution, or even that all the ideology shaping the prerevolutionary controversy was constitutional. Rather, to the extent that the causes of the Revolution were ideological, and to the extent that ideology was constitutional, this study contends that the ideological school has misled us by reading the constitutional out of the story.

To emphasize the constitutional origins of the American Revolution does not deny the validity of much of the work by historians who have followed a different theory. In fact, it enforces many of the historical hypotheses that have been advanced by connecting those hypotheses to eighteenth-century thought. Consider:

1. The constitutional emphasis does not require that either imperial or continental politics be treated as more important than local politics. It provides, rather, new vitality to local origins by explaining how town meetings and county associations, as far apart as New Hampshire and Georgia, and not in contact with one another, used similar language to enunciate similar principles and responded uniformly to perceived political dangers. They did so because eighteenth-century Americans everywhere had internalized the same constitutional program.

2. The constitutional perspective sheds new light on the long exploded thesis that the American Revolution was fought to settle two questions: the question of home rule and the question of who should rule at home. It restates the question by taking eighteenth-century concerns into account and concludes that the Americans sought the same rule at home as their fellow subjects enjoyed in Great Britain—the rule of law.

3. The constitutional emphasis does not dispute the "imperialist" thesis that American colonial history can be understood only as part of the larger history of the eighteenth-century British empire. It explains, rather, the principles and ideals uniting the peripheries to the center.[33]

4. Although the constitutional emphasis disproves the thesis of those progressive historians who, in the early decades of this century, disparaged the American whigs by depicting them as hypocrites, attempting to hide their ecomonic motivations behind a mask of constitutionalism, it does not eschew economic considerations. It explains why even the most militant colonial whigs would have left control of the economy to Great Britain, not even asking that trade be regulated either reasonably or equally, but, on their part, "cheerfully" consenting to acts of Parliament "securing the commercial advantages of the whole Empire to the mother country."[34]

5. The constitutional emphasis sheds light on some doubts raised by a school of British historians of the eighteenth century led by Sir Lewis Namier. They questioned the sincerity of the support for American rights voiced by the British opposition. Virtually no one in British politics, the

Namierists contended, had any political principles that reached beyond
local or factional interests. "The argument, though convincingly presented,
presumes a consistent hypocrisy or delusion on the part of the [British]
Whig opposition," Edmund S. Morgan has pointed out. "It may be that the
Whigs were hypocritical in their attack on George III and their support of
the Americans. But if so why were they hypocritical in just the way they
were? Why did they appeal to principles of government that later won
acceptance?"[35] The answer in most instances is that the British opposition
was arguing for the same constitution that the Americans were defending.
Their economic interests and political goals may not have been the same as
those of colonial whigs, but because they were arguing the same constitutional law, their rhetoric was the same.[36]

6. The constitutional emphasis does not negate the recent scholarship on
republicanism. It clarifies it. Much of the rhetoric attributed to republicanism comes straight out of the literature of the common law, from the writings of Sir Edward Coke, Sir Matthew Hale, and even Sir William Blackstone. Scholars must pay more heed to the connection between law and
virtue. Legal language was the founders' chief tool for crafting their new
civic world. The security of constitutionalism through the rule of law provided the vocabulary not just for revolution, but for constructing the framework of virtue. Republicanism is, in large part, constitutionalism recycled
under another label.

7. Finally, the constitutional perspective was an important motivation for
those Americans who opposed the Stamp Act on the streets of Boston in
1765 and who fought the British army at Yorktown in 1781. As Page Smith
observed: "After a century and a half of progress in historical scholarship, in
research techniques, in tools and methods, we have found our way to the
interpretation held, substantially, by those historians who themselves partic-
ipated in or lived through the era of the Revolution."[37]

JURISPRUDENTIAL PREFACE

To understand the constitutional debates leading up to the American Revolution we must think as participants in that debate thought. If we are to do that, if we are to think as people in the eighteenth century thought about law, we must appreciate the meanings and the nuances of words such as "arbitrary," "constitutional," "legal," and "political."

"Arbitrary" is an especially challenging word. A conclusion to be drawn from this book is that the American constitutional case against the authority of Parliament to legislate for the internal policies of the colonies depended to a large extent on the illegitimacy of arbitrary power in English and British constitutional theory. Dissentient lords summed up the legal doctrine when they described the Port of Boston Act—a parliamentary statute punishing Boston for destroying British owned property at the Boston Tea Party—as "an arbitrary Sentence" and protested that the length of the sentence was left to the arbitrary discretion of the minister advising the crown if and when Boston had satisfied the penalty. In a concise statement of the constitutional principle, they asserted, "The legal Condition of the Subject (standing unattainted by Conviction for Treason or Felony) ought never to depend upon the arbitrary Will of any Person whatsoever."[1] That single sentence not only invokes a legal principle dominating much of English constitutional history, but sums up much of the American whig constitutional case against Parliament's authority to legislate.

"Constitutional" is a less difficult word. People in the eighteenth century thought of constitutionalism somewhat differently than people today think of constitutionalism. For one thing, they thought of it more often. "Perhaps never before and surely never since," it recently was said, "has any single nation's constitution so dominated Western man's theorizing about politics."[2] Indeed, the British constitution dominated theorizing not only about politics, but about the purview of law and the trappings of government.[3]

Again, pay heed to words. In a constitutional history of the eighteenth century it is not nitpicking to do what many students of the eighteenth century fail to do, and distinguish the words "law" and "constitution" from the word "politics." Quite often scholars of the American Revolution use "political" when "constitutional" would be more descriptive, and do not differentiate between "constitutional" and "legal." Drawing distinctions between "constitutional" and "political" or between "constitution" and "law" is usually unnecessary, for the meaning is generally clear, but if we seek the precision of pellucid usage, the distinction can be valuable. To leave lines uncertain runs the risk that concepts will become blurred. It is through words that we convey meaning, and the words "constitutional" and "legal" do not always conjure up the same concepts.

When one looks back two hundred years, there is a tendency to compound what was then "law" with what is now "constitution," or, too often, to project the precision of today's terms back on the relativity of eighteenth-century constitutionality, and thus conjoin what was legal in eighteenth-century Great Britain with what is constitutional in twentieth-century United States. For an eighteenth-century jurisprude to argue that standing armies were unconstitutional in Great Britain was not to argue that they were illegal. That would be a conclusion peculiar to Americans, an error that British or Canadian citizens would be less likely to make. What the judiciary in twentieth-century United States rule unconstitutional is, *ipso facto*, illegal. The meaning of law and constitution was markedly different in the eighteenth century, just as it is today in Canada. "In our usage," an Ontario court has explained, "that is unconstitutional which is opposed to the principles, more or less vaguely and generally stated, upon which we think the people should be governed; in the American sense, it is that which transgresses the written document called the 'Constitution.' With us anything unconstitutional is wrong, though it may be legal; with them, it is illegal, though it may be right. Accordingly, to say that a measure is unconstitutional does not with us indicate anything as to its legality."[4] When eighteenth-century British or Americans, therefore, made the claim that standing armies were unconstitutional, they did not mean that the existing British army was unlawful. Of course it was legal; it had been sanctioned by Parliament. But Parliament's promulgation only made law, it did not resolve questions of constitutionality. The relativeness of the concept "constitutional" in the eighteenth century may be difficult for Americans to comprehend today, but then it made legal sense to say that while the people's militia was "a more frugal and constitutional measure than a Standing Army," the navy was "the most constitutional force" of all. The army, militia, and navy were equally legal, but not equally constitutional.[5]

The other conceptual arrangement of historical material that should be distinguished from "constitutional" is "political." To compound "political" with "constitutional" is not necessarily an error. It may, however, be a matter of changing the emphasis of the revolutionary debate from an eighteenth-century to a twentieth-century context. In the eighteenth century the word "constitutional" was much broader in meaning than it is in today's United States, but narrower than the word "political." The same was true for some usages of the word "law." "The very Idea of Law," Edmund Burke told the House of Commons, was "to exclude the discretion in the Judge."[6] According to eighteenth-century definitions, the "political" or politics (which included much law that was promulgated by legislation rather than by the courts or by custom) was programmed by interest, will, party, desire, benefit, or need. Law (including that higher or restraining aspect of law, constitutional law) was guided by neutrality, analogy, continuity, precedent, maxim, and custom. In the eighteenth century, to describe a course of action as "constitutional" was to say that to take that action would be to proceed in conformity to law, in conformity to custom, and in conformity to the current arrangement of constitutional conventions. Deviation from that course of action would be legally inadvisable, contrary to established custom, and not in conformity to the current arrangement of governmental conventions. For a person to assert that an action was "constitutional" was to associate that action with customary practice, at least to the extent that it was in accord with the operational tradition of certain official institutions and could be justified as consistent with that tradition. To assert that an action was "political" was to say it was a matter of choice rather than precedent, that it was selected from a number of options, and more likely was a decision for this day or this generation, not for all ages and all generations. As a result, the formulation of argument was quite different. In the eighteenth century what was perceived as "constitutional" was argued in terms of principle, parity, doctrine, continuity, disinterest, and "right." What was perceived as "political" was argued in terms of program, result, policy, command, choice, and "power."

These distinctions—"constitutional," "legal," and "political"—should be kept in mind when considering the scope of this book. It is concerned only with the *constitutional* aspects of the American Revolution, not with its *social* causes, *political* origins, *economic* history, or *nationalistic* motivations. Another topic that is not covered is the *legal* history of the Revolution, thus eliminating large areas of historical discussion about eighteenth-century law—questions, issues, and disputes more properly belonging to legal than to constitutional history. Among the most obvious of these are controversies, regulations, and subterfuges associated with the Navigation Act and other laws of trade, or the conditions of local law in the American colonies that made ineffectual or even nullified the mandates of imperial British law and the usefulness of the British army.[7]

CONSTITUTIONAL
HISTORY OF THE
AMERICAN REVOLUTION

ABRIDGED EDITION

CHAPTER ONE

THE AUTHORITY OF THE CONSTITUTION

Unlike the American state and federal constitutions, the British constitution was never written; it was not a set of directives adopted by the people granting government its prerogatives and limiting its powers. The British constitution, rather, was an idea, a way of thinking and arguing about authority, an outline of governmental goals and principles derived from existing institutions, laws, and customs, and drawn by deduction from the patterns by which they functioned. More to the point, the unwritten British constitution was an apparatus of limitation, a restraint on command, both the source of definition of individual civil rights and the chief protector of those rights.

English-speaking people in the eighteenth century judged the legitimacy of the British constitution by how well it secured the person of the individual citizen and that citizen's civil rights. "[A] Constitution in its Proper Idea," the freeholders of Concord, Massachusetts, voted in 1776, "intends a System of Principles Established to Secure the Subject[s] in the Possession and enjoyment of their Rights and Priviliges [sic], against any Encroachments of the Governing part." "A good constitution," the Reverend Ebenezer Bridge had told Massachusetts lawmakers nine years earlier, is one "that secures the mutual dependence of the sovereign or ruling powers, and the people on each other, and which secures the rights of each, and the good of the whole society."[1]

3

Two concepts pervaded eighteenth-century British constitutionalism. One was limitation. Constitutional government was limited government. The second was security. In fact, some legal theorists defined "constitution" as security of rights. "The British constitution is made to secure liberty and property," *Demophoon* told London's *Political Register*, "whatever takes away these, takes away the constitution itself, and cannot be constitutional." That statement by *Demophoon* reveals yet another eighteenth-century definition of "constitutionalism." An act of power jeopardizing security was not "constitutional." David Hartley, who was negotiator for Great Britain of the treaty ending the American Revolution, referred to that meaning of constitutionalism when observing that a "limited excise" (that is, one affecting only vendors of the product being taxed) "may be called a constitutional excise," but a "general excise" (one permitting revenue agents to enter the private houses of users of the product being taxed) "is unconstitutional." The first was "consistent with the liberty of the subject," the second "totally repugnant to the freedom of our constitution."[2]

Eighteenth-century constitutionalism was as positive as it was negative. By the very process of limiting government it created rights. "A *constitution* is the *organization of the contributed rights* in society," Pennsylvania's John Dickinson theorized. "GOVERNMENT is the EXERCISE of them. It is intended for the benefit of *the governed*; of course [it] can have no just powers but what conduce to *that end*." Indeed, there were even writers who used the word "constitution" as if its meaning was limited to the security of citizens and their rights, implying either that the constitution was nothing less than a collection of individual rights, or that its chief function was to protect rights.[3]

This is not the place to enumerate the rights protected by the eighteenth-century British constitution.[4] Here we are concerned with constitutional doctrine, and to pursue that topic attention must be given to the most striking peculiarity of that constitution—the dichotomy of the two constitutions. We should not be surprised that many scholars have missed the two constitutions when we realize contemporaries paid the dichotomy slight heed. Lawyers and members of Parliament, London imperialists, and American whigs argued constitutional principles as if dealing with a single, familiar, fixed constitutional theory. In truth, however, the British constitution throughout the eighteenth century was in a remarkable state of contrariety—not a state of transition, it is always in such a state, but a state of polarity. Constitutional theory in Great Britain was torn between competing constitutional doctrines which, without tearing the nation into governmental impotency, existed side by side, each supported by tenable, familiar, aggressive legal theories. Indeed, the eighteenth century can be termed the epoch of two constitutions in both Great Britain and the American colonies,[5] with the mother country eventually succumbing to the obvious convenience of one constitution and the independent American states consciously selecting the other.

If one wishes to summarize the dichotomy in two sentences, it could be said that British imperialists had moved away from the traditional constitutionalist theory that England had been governed from time immemorial by the same "ancient constitution."[6] They were, instead, "looking ahead" to the British constitution of today, to government by representational consent, to a constitution of parliamentary command, in which government exercises arbitrary power and the civil rights of citizens are grants conferred at the discretion of the sovereign. The Americans were "looking backward," not to a government by popular consent but to government by the rule of law, to a sovereign that did not grant rights but was limited by rights, and that was the creature rather than the creator of law, (with law the guardian of liberty).

It may be that we have forgotten that second constitution, the backward-looking American constitution of prescriptive, customary rights. Scholars of the American Revolution have uniformly interpreted the constitutional controversy in terms of the "forward-looking" constitution of sovereign command. It is, after all, easier to understand—law was the command of the sovereign, with the British Parliament the sovereign—and based on a jurisprudence most know, for ever since the middle of the nineteenth century law in the English-speaking world has been command. Historians tend to project the law with which they are familiar back on earlier legal systems and students of the Revolution have been no exception. There is an imbalance to the story that must be redressed by rediscovering the premises of that other constitutional theory, the constitution of customary rights. Under this constitution law was not command, but was groped by arguing natural law, community consensus, right reason, established usage, precedential evidence, implied contracts, collective ownership, and, most importantly, customary practice.

The Authority of Custom: By the tenets of custom in the eighteenth century, whatever had been done in the nation or community from time immemorial was constitutional and legal. Whatever consciously had been abstained from in the nation or community from time immemorial was unconstitutional or illegal. Immemorial time was a relevant segment of time during which the memory of the law did not show a contrary custom. From the perspective of custom the constitution was a collection of legal principles established through the discovery of precedential usages. It was, in other words, a combination of: 1) inductive revelation drawn from appropriate principles by examining past experiences; and 2) deductive application of these principles to current constitutional issues. The eighteenth-century legal mind assumed a universally known constitutional law existing independent of will or command for which custom was the best evidence.

Keep in mind two preliminary points when evaluating custom as authority for constitutional law in the eighteenth century: 1) that law *qua* custom was positive law and must not be confused with natural law; and 2) that custom informed law on several levels. On the most elementary level, custom told law which rules and procedures operated successfully. We may be amazed, but eighteenth-century constitutional theory thought custom both safer than command (whether promulgated by crown or legislature) and more certain to beget better law. It was safer, common lawyers contended, because unlike sovereign's command it did not "judge individuals upon laws occasionally enacted, and arising suddenly out of the heat of the times, or the peculiar circumstances of the case under contemplation." It was better than legislation in several ways. One advantage was that, spawned by the common people, it was less arbitrary than legislative command. A usage's survival over several generations proved its utility and popular consent. It was through custom, Bishop Gilbert Burnet argued, that "the common sense of all Men [gives] a just and good Title." It also gave law more than a touch of democracy without the bother of a democratic government. The theory was never better explained than by an Anglo-Irish judge a century and a half before the American Revolution: "When a reasonable act once done is found to be good and beneficial to the people, and agreeable to their nature and disposition, then do they use it and practise it again and again, and so by often iteration and multiplication of the act it becometh a *Custome*; and being continued without interruption time out of mind, it obtaineth the force of a *Law*."[7]

Custom had many facets. Custom was law's evidence, one of the chief sources for the authority of law and, as authority, was in fact law. Thomas Wood stated the rule in his *Institute of the Laws*: usage and ancient custom make law. There were even law writers in the eighteenth century who thought custom held more authority than parliamentary command. "[S]o great and omnipotent is the power of custom," a pamphleteer wrote in 1764, "that it not only creates laws, but has produced a Court, whose decisions controul, and render inoperative and of non-effect, acts authorised by the express words of the Legislative Power." He meant the Court of Chancery, "whose jurisdiction is solely founded on custom."[8]

At the time of the English Civil War a royalist judge could claim that Charles I was entitled to "that which all his Ancestors, Kings of this Realm, have enjoyed: That enjoyment and usage makes the *Law*." One of the constitutional issues of the American Revolution was whether that rule was still true for the British constitution. Certainly it was for local colonial constitutions. All colonial constitutional procedures and many colonial constitutional rights were derived from custom, particularly legislative privileges and the criterion for legislative representation. The writer of a 1767

London political pamphlet relied on the authority of custom when telling George Grenville that, although Americans were not represented in Parliament, they had "from their very first establishment, for more than 100 years, uniformly exercised and enjoyed the privilege of imposing and raising their own taxes, in their provincial assemblies, of which they choose the members. So that they look upon themselves now to be not only intitled thereto by the principles of the *British* government, but by an uninterrupted usage sufficient of itself to make a constitution."[9]

If we are to understand the constitutional controversy leading to the American Revolution we must appreciate the function of custom in eighteenth-century jurisprudence. Of all the sources of British constitutionalism, custom was the most important. No other doctrine of constitutional authority, not even the concept of the original contract, had as strong a hold on the English and American legal mind as the authority of custom. It is too often loosely disparaged today, either because it is believed to have been easily manipulated, or because it is, mistakenly, thought to have been a constitutional device for defending the status quo.

There is no denying that custom was pliable. Like decisional law today custom could usually be found to support most positions, and, if not, something could be concocted. It is not true, however, that custom served the status quo as that charge is understood today. The chief function of custom before the nineteenth century was to restrain power. It was not helpful to arbitrary command; it was an instrument for constitutionalism, not a device for extending prerogative rule. Indeed, far from thinking of custom as a servant of the status quo, the eighteenth century thought of it more as the guarantor of political neutrality. Immanent, unmade, and rooted in the past, custom was thought to be independent of human judgment and human choice, not only relatively neutral but politically benign, the legal opposite of the feared bane of constitutionalism, sovereign command. To the extent that custom involved choice, the choice seemed to come from many generations and many minds, not from one generation or one mind. "A system of civil and political government," an Irish writer explained in 1783, "the fundamental principles of which are certain immemorial usages, whose antiquity, if other proofs were wanting, speaks their superior wisdom; and certain memorable precedents, in which the just and virtuous struggles of our ancestors, recognized as just and virtuous by the common consent of successive generations, point out to their posterity how we too ought to act under similar circumstances."[10]

No one expressed more confidence in the neutrality of custom than the greatest of the eighteenth-century parliamentarians, Edmund Burke. For him custom's neutrality did more than guarantee constitutionalism by securing property and government. It secured law itself. "[T]his is a choice, not of one day, or one set of people, not a tumultuary and giddy choice; it is a deliberate election of ages and generations; it is a constitution made by what is ten thousand times better than choice, it is made by the peculiar circumstances, occasions, tempers, dispositions, and moral, civil and social habitudes of the people, which disclose themselves only in a long space of time."[11]

The authority of ownership: There is a prejudice in the late twentieth century against equating protection of material goods with a civil right that has led to a misunderstanding of eighteenth-century legal terminology. The thought has been that when seventeenth-century English or eighteenth-century Americans defended the concept of irrevocable ownership in property, they were speaking as a governing class seeking to safeguard their private possessions, both personal and real. Sometimes they were, and there is no need to ignore that fact. But in eighteenth-century legal terminology, the word "property" embraced more than physical objects. Property was also the interest or dominion lawfully held over the object; a species of title, inchoate or complete, legal or equitable, corporeal or incorporeal, tangible or intangible, visible or invisible, real, personal, or contractual. In constitutional terminology "property" referred to the object but the object was intangible, a legal abstraction. Most commonly, in revolutionary constitutional debates "property" referred to civic privileges of all kinds. When people in the eighteenth century spoke of constitutional safeguards protecting "life, liberty, and property" they were referring to such intangibles as the right to jury trial, the right to petition government, and the right to the constitution itself. The constitutional issue to be discussed in the next chapter, the right to be taxed only by yourself or your representative, was, the *New London Gazette*, asserted, "a fundamental birth-right-privilege." These rights were *owned*, they were constitutional rights that were property, and that attribute—being *property*—provided the constitutional standing to shield them from the capriciousness of arbitrary governmental action.[12]

The language of property, as employed by common lawyers, was accepted idiom in popular political discussion because, when property was mentioned, the issues were generally constitutional. "Have the two Houses [of Parliament] a strict right & property to lay upon the people what Taxes they shall judge meet?" the royalist jurist David Jenkins had asked in 1648, using the concept of property to measure the power of government. "Have the parliament a *right* to take from the lowest of the subjects the smallest privilege which he inherits, unless forfeited by law?" Nicholas Ray asked in 1765, reversing the ownership and vesting the property in the subject. In both instances, "property" served as restraint upon government. An inherited privilege may not strike us today as a civil right or an entitlement, but in 1765 it was properly thought of as property because the operating concept was ownership.[13]

There were numerous ways to express that ownership, yet always it seems to have been done with terms lifted from the vocabulary of the common law. "Freehold" was one word. A familiar way of expressing the authority of ownership was to say, "our Liberties are our Freehold." Another word was "estate." To assert that people had an "estate" in constitutional rights was so common it would be redundant to quote an example. Unique enough to justify quotation, however, is a sentence written by Sir John Hawles demonstrating the flexibility of constitutional language by converting the noun into a verb. Hawles wrote of "the true Liberties and Priviledges which every *English man* is Justly Intituled unto, and Estated in by his Birth-right."[14]

There were two words used more frequently than any others to describe the authority of constitutional ownership. One was "birthright" and the other was "inheritance." "We have a right to petition; that is the birth-right of Englishmen," the lord mayor of London boasted in 1770. "I am restored to my birthright, to the noble liberties and privileges of an Englishman," a future lord mayor, John Wilkes, announced on being released from king's bench prison. Birth was the source explaining the authority. The British were said to have a right to liberty "from birth." A person owned the security of constitutionalism just by being born British. William Penn entitled one of his pamphlets, *The Most Excellent Privilege of Liberty & Property Being the Birth-Right of the Freeborn Subjects of England*.[15]

"Inheritance," the other common ownership word, was not a different concept from "birthright" but another way of stating the authority of ownership conferred by birth. The right of liberty provides a good example of a right inherited. "Liberty . . . is your inheritance," Charles Lucas assured Dubliners. "The Common Law," Sir Edward Coke told the Petition of Right Commons, "hath so admeasured the Kings Prerogative, as he cannot prejudice any man in his inheritance, and the greatest inheritance a man hath is the liberty of his person, for all others are accessary to it." Liberty, William Penn contended, was the "inestimable Inheritance that every Free-born Subject of England is Heir unto by Birthright."[16]

To speak of an inherited birthright in constitutionalism was an old established—one might almost say *inherited*—method of pleading to the constitutional merits. "[T]he liberties, franchises, privileges, and jurisdiction of parliament are the ancient and undoubted birthright and inheritance of the subjects of England," the Commons reminded Charles I in 1628. Thirteen years later, the Irish Commons claimed "their Birthright and best Inheritance" in a protest against Strafford's regime, and sixteen years after that it was the interregnum Commons protesting to Oliver Cromwell that their "liberties and privileges" were "the birth-right and inheritance of the people."[17]

The authority of purchase: It is not a favorable comment on our times that twentieth-century scholars have removed themselves so far from eighteenth-century constitutionalism they are peeved by the idea of property as a civil right. Of course, there is the risk of misunderstanding when language is unexpected. Eighteenth-century Britons, drawing on an ancient vocabulary of constitutionalism, used expressions to claim constitutional rights that would not occur to us. They spoke of constitutional principles that were "the Purchase of the People" obtained with "valuable Considerations," "the Purchase of their Ancestors, as a gracious and royal Reward of the Merit and Services of their Forefathers, and as one of the best Inheritances they left to their Children," and of "those rights and immunities which were purchased for us, by the lives and blood of our worthy ancestors, and secured to us by solemn stipulation (or contract) with our late majesties King William and Queen Mary." When used by colonial whigs these words have misled some students of the American Revolution. They have dismissed the language of purchase as American bombast, at best bogus claims to bogus rights for which there was no constitutional authority and which could be supported only by passionate tales of heroic ancestors.[18]

When Americans claimed that their ancestors had "purchased" their right to constitutionalism through the costs of settlement or by the sacrifice of lives fighting Indians, we reasonably might guess they had developed an original legal theory. We would be wrong. Seventeenth-century English commonwealthmen had made the same argument in their struggles against the House of Stuart, as had the Anglo-Irish in their fight to keep the English and British parliaments from exercising sovereign power over Ireland. Indeed, unfamiliar as the American whig language may sound to us, contemporaries in the mother country used exactly the same words when formulating constitutional authority for their civil rights and privileges. A word charged with legal meaning then was "blood." An authority cited for the right to be governed by constitutional restraints was that "our ancestors redeemed" those rights "with their blood," "sealed with their blood," "purchased for us with their blood," or "purchased with seas of blood, to entail our posterity."[19]

Blood had more meaning than we would think. To "seal with blood" and "entail our posterity" were not rhetorical flourishes inserted in petitions to grab attention. Like the Anglo-Irish before them, the chief claim by American whigs of purchasing constitutional rights was not by paying money to natives for sovereignty but by undergoing the financial costs and physical dangers of migration. Even if the colonists did not have a right to liberty by other constitutional authority, John Adams explained, "our fathers have earned it and bought it for us, at the expence of their ease, their estates, their pleasure and their blood." They had done it by migration, the people of Salem were told in 1768, when "they undauntedly exposed themselves to every kind of hardship, and bravely met death in the high places of the field, that they might secure to you a quiet possession of those rights and liberties, which as men, as Englishmen, and as Christians, they knew you were entitled to."[20]

The constitutional theory may no longer be persuasive but it was descended from an ancient and legitimate lineage. Generations of English citizens had pleaded constitutional restraints limiting the power of their kings on the grounds that they and their ancestors had made sacrifices for him and his ancestors, generally by spilling their blood. It is simply wrong to say, therefore, as it was said in 1976, that when towns in revolutionary New England passed resolutions reciting the dangers and bravery of the first generation that they were boasting that "their ancestors had been heroes." They were, rather, explaining an authority—purchase—upon which they based part of their claim to be governed by constitutional principles. It is for that reason that clergymen preached of "dearly purchased privileges," of "valuable, dear-bought rights," of "liberties" that "our fathers dearly bought" and that "descend to us in a patrimony purchased at their expense," and of "the dear bought patrimony of our pious, noble spirited ancestors, which they have procured for us, at an immense cost of treasure and blood." These clergymen were boasting of constitutionalism purchased, not of ancestors to be praised.[21]

It is worth considering that in Great Britain this language was not confined to popular political pamphlets. It was familiar fare in official resolutions and appeared in petitions to Parliament. London's Common Council, for example, warned King George III of "the desperate Attempts which have been, and are too successfully made . . . to subvert those sacred Laws which our Ancestors have sealed with their Blood." And in words reminiscent of many American petitions, the East India Company protested legislation that intruded upon its corporate autonomy, by saying it was "subversive of those rights which they [the company] held under their charter; the original privileges of which, in the continuation thereof, have been purchased by their predecessors from the public for a valuable consideration, and repeatedly confirmed by several acts of parliament." The legal principle was that constitutional protections had been acquired by "purchase," and rested on the authority of implied contract and prescriptive custom. That was the meaning of the earl of Chatham when he told the House of Lords of America's "dear-bought privileges," and what London's Council was thinking of when it told the Commons that the East India Bill would, if enacted, destroy "the most sacred rights of the subject, purchased for a valuable consideration, and sanctioned by the most *solemn charters* and *acts of parliament.*"[22]

The authority of precedent: One reason the East India Bill threatened "the most sacred rights of the subject" was the doctrine of precedent—if enacted it could become a precedent for similar legislation of arbitrary command. At its weakest, the doctrine of precedent did not furnish constitutional authority but was merely advisory. That sort of precedent served "not to promote but [to] check Innovation," Lord Mulgrave explained in 1769, "by warning" legislators "to be extremely cautious, and maturely to consider the Expediency of any Step which their Ancestors have never found it necessary to take." At its strongest, precedent was binding law, as Nathaniel Forster indicated when arguing that the expulsion of Sir Robert Walpole by the House of Commons was a precedent proving the constitutional authority of the Commons to bar the reelection of John Wilkes as member for Middlesex after he had been expelled by vote of the house. "What ever doubt then there might have been in law before Mr. Walpole's case," Forster wrote, "there can be none now. The decision of the house upon this case is strictly in point, to prove, that expulsion creates absolute incapacity in law of being reelected." The authority was even stronger if the precedent was specific legislation, especially a tax, for which there had been no precedent. Before that new tax was enacted, and because Parliament had never before imposed such a tax, the argument could be made either that it lacked authority to do so or that the tax would be unconstitutional. With enactment, however, these arguments would lose much constitutional persuasion—especially if the tax was paid without protest by some of the people being taxed. That legislation was now precedent for the authority to enact future taxes of an analogous nature. Precedent making was a consequence of law making that eighteenth-century legislators were regularly urged to keep in mind. After the ministry announced in 1763 that Parliament would impose an unprecedented excise on cider and perry, an opponent warned that "if this new extension of the Excise-laws is confirmed, it must effectually justify and authorise every future extension of them which can be proposed, till the Excise becomes general." To say there was no limit to where a precedent might lead was not a political prediction. It was constitutional doctrine, an explanation of law. Two years later Prime Minister George Grenville asked former Attorney General Charles Yorke for a legal opinion on the proposed American Stamp Act. "The precedent may," Yorke replied, "be in argument extended far, to other future taxes, upon the colonies."[23]

Besides statutory precedents there were other kinds of precedents argued during the revolutionary controversy, precedents of a sort no longer known in twentieth-century law, which can be called "precedents of history." These range from the very general to the very particular. The general consisted of broad, assumptive claims as, for example, assertions that were central to the British side of the American revolutionary controversy—that Parliament could constitutionally legislate for the colonies because Americans "never disputed" the authority of Parliament to bind by legislation "in all cases whatsoever," or that "[t]he Supremacy" of Parliament had always been "acknowledged" by Americans. The facts that Americans had never denied but may have acknowledged parliamentary supremacy were broad, general precedents providing some not very persuasive support of parliamentary supremacy. The more particular "precedents of history" relied on specific statements from the past, incidents that had happened or events that had not occurred, and civic practices supposedly delineating attitudes of officials either at home or in the colonies. An example occurred when the Massachusetts General Court convened in 1769 at a moment of imperial crisis, with both houses determined to demand removal of British troops from the colony and to challenge the supremacy of Parliament. Before beginning the session, however, all members swore the oath of allegiance "required by Act of Parliament." Just taking that oath, Governor Thomas Hutchinson argued, created a precedent acknowledging Parliament's supremacy. "Shall we now dispute," he asked, "whether Acts of Parliament have been submitted to in Points which are the very Essence of our Constitution?"[24]

Today it is difficult to understand Hutchinson's argument. Precedents from history are now virtually unknown in either British or American constitutional law. They were a strategy peculiar to the advocacy of an unwritten constitution of customary rights, an argumentative tool for setting the limits of a precedential constitution. We must keep them in mind for historical precedents were argued by everyone during the American revolutionary controversy—even by adherents to the constitution of sovereign command who claimed that by inherent constitutional right Parliament could bind the colonies in all cases whatsoever, yet, somewhat inconsistently, did not scruple to prove Parliament's authority by historical precedent.

The authority of nature: It is hardly surprising that jurisprudes of the constitution of sovereign command, trained in eighteenth-century law, lapsed into the theory of the constitution of customary rights. What may be surprising is that subsequent historians of the nineteenth and twentieth centuries had done the same, some even using precedents of history to reach conclusions about the history they write. Sir David Lindsay Keir, a British constitutional historian, claimed that historical precedents proved that American whigs were wrong on the law. "Their [constitutional] case was fatally impaired," Keir concluded, "by the undeniable fact that the authority of numerous British statutes (including some, like the Bill of Rights, which might almost be regarded as integral to their own case) had long been accepted by them as binding. Their only course was to appeal to natural justice, which removed the question from the sphere of constitutional law."[25]

Keir made three points. First, that Parliament gained a historical precedent proving its authority to bind the colonies by legislation every time an American government acknowledged the binding force of any parliamentary statute.[26] Second, Keir claimed—and American whigs would have agreed—that natural law was different from British constitutional law. Third, he said that because American whigs lost their constitutional case they were driven to natural law.

There may be no other legal assertion more frequently argued by American revolutionaries than that, after discovering that the contemporary British constitution did not support their case against Parliament's claim to authority to bind them by legislation in all cases whatsoever, they were forced to justify rebellion by appealing to "the rights of men in general" or to "natural law." The chief evidence proving this assertion is supposedly the Declaration of Independence. For example, Charles Howard McIlwain, in a book concerned with the constitutional history of the American Revolution, argued that the Declaration of Independence was "based on the law of nature instead of the constitution of the British Empire." And Carl Becker, in a very influential but remarkably simplistic study of the Declaration of Independence, asserted that it denounced "George III to a 'candid world' for his violation of the natural rights of man." That assertion has become one of the most widely repeated errors of American history. Anyone giving a reasonable reading to the entire Declaration of Independence, not just to the rhetorical preamble where "nature and nature's God" are mentioned, will readily see that that document accused the king of Great Britain of violating only the legal and constitutional rights of American colonists. It did not, in a single instance, accuse George III of violating a natural right. In fact, natural law was never cited by an official colonial governmental body to identify a right claimed, except rights that were also claimed as constitutional rights. Natural law simply was not a significant part of the American whig constitutional case; certainly not nearly as important as some twentieth-century writers have assumed.[27]

This is not the place to measure the irrelevance of natural law to the American Revolution controversy.[28] Two points may be mentioned to sum up the evidence why natural law has been overemphasized in the historical literature. First, it was common practice in the eighteenth century to couple appeals to natural law with positive-law authority such as the British constitution, the English constitution, the American constitution, the colonial charters, the original contract, Magna Carta, the Bill of Rights, or common law. Even eighteenth-century jurists who contended that "natural rights" existed on their own authority, and most did, usually tied them to "constitutional rights." Almost universally, scholars of later generations have discounted the constitutional or legal references, dismissing them as strategic window dressing or ignoring them completely. In 1768, for example, James

DeLancey moved in the New York assembly that the British Mutiny Act was a "high enfringement of the freedom of the inhabitants of this Colony and tends to deprive them of their natural and constitutional rights and privileges." Referring to this motion, a historian noted that DeLancey's party won the next election and concluded that "Captain DeLancey's bold attack on the authority of Parliament and in the name of human rights had clearly not hurt his faction." The appeal to constitutional rights, apparently, was immaterial.[29]

Second, natural rights were not based on the authority of nature alone. Appeals to natural law during the eighteenth century more often than not were appeals to constitutional law or to positive law. The town of Boston spoke of "the undoubted natural Rights of Subjects," and we think the reference is to natural law. Instead, Boston's "undoubted natural Rights" were rights "declared in the aforesaid Act of Parliament," that is the English bill of rights. Boston's natural rights, then, were not abstract rights received by the authority of nature, but specific rights, grounded in constitutional legislation. In 1768, the Virginia House of Burgesses claimed that "their ancestors brought over with them intire, and transmitted to their descendants, the natural and constitutional rights they had enjoyed in their native country." Rather than detailing these rights or indicating in what natural phenomenon they would be found, the Virginians said that these "natural and constitutional rights" meant "a legislative authority . . . derived, and assimilated as nearly as might be to that of England." If that was what "natural and constitutional rights" meant, they could have more accurately been called "constitutional rights" only. Almost invariably, when one examines texts cited as evidence that natural law was the authority of revolutionary American legal claims, they prove to contain the phase "natural and constitutional," and depend on constitutional law alone.[30]

The authority of contract: With the exception of custom, there was no concept more important in shaping the American revolutionary constitutional argument than the concept of contract. Contract was the heart of the American case because, again with the exception of custom, it was the heart of traditional English and British constitutionalism. In seventeenth-century Great Britain, many political theories and almost all constitutional theory were shaped by contractarian thought. It was adaptable to every issue and was a standard that could be used to judge every problem. During the revolutionary controversy both sides—even adherents of the constitution of sovereign command—appealed to contractarian theory, making similar constitutional arguments for similar constitutional reasons.

"[O]ur forefathers," the people of the town of Weymouth, Massachusetts, lamented shortly before the Stamp Act was to become operative, "have told us that they should never have left the land of their nativity, and fled to these ends of the earth, triumph'd over dangers, encountered difficulties innumerable, and suffer'd hardships unparallel'd, but for the sake of securely enjoying civil and religious liberty, and that the same might be transmitted safe to their posterity."[31]

It would be grievous error to associate the argument with John Locke. His theory of the social contract and its influence on the political philosophy of American whigs has too long been overemphasized. Whig reliance on a constitutional compact rested on the firmer ground of the original contract. Too often in our own times students of the American Revolution have encountered a contractarian argument and without reflection have assumed John Locke's influence, and the original contract has been mistaken for and compounded with the social contract.

The social contract was a legal fiction explaining the conditions under which individuals left the state of nature and created societies. The constitutional or government contract—called the original contract in the eighteenth century—was an implied agreement between ruler and ruled from which the powers and limitations of government were inferred. The first is a theory of the origin of society, the second a theory of the constitution of government. It would be unnecessary even to mention the social contract had it not been treated as significant by twentieth-century commentators confusing it with the original contract, a mistake seldom committed in the eighteenth century. After the Revolution had begun and Americans, creating new political arrangements, had to think of the nature of society, the social contract assumed some importance in both constitutional and political theory. That period and those issues should not be confused with the revolutionary controversy. The social contract had a place in the debates over constitution making. It played no role in the debates about the constitutional authority of the British Parliament. By contrast, no legal concept save the doctrine of custom was more important to the revolutionary debates than the original contract.

Unlike the social contract, the original contract did not depend on theories about the need of humans to escape the state of nature. It was implied from historical events and based on principles of government that the person citing the contract either wanted continued or hoped to establish. It would be wrong, therefore, to think of legal fictions or of constitutional subterfuge. The original contract was much more real than the twentieth century is willing to credit. As late as 1992 a writer described contractarian argument as "modern," a development of the "radicalism" of the American Revolution which supplanted "the traditional patriarchal idea of authority." That writer was imposing twentieth-century suppositions on eighteenth-century constitutional concepts. Seen from a less speculative perspective, that is, as seen through eighteenth-century suppositions, the original contract was an ancient constitutional doctrine which for centuries had been employed as a foresenic argument restraining power, while patriarchalism, like republicanism, is modern theory invented to accommodate an otherwise insupportable historical thesis.[32] The concept of contract was an apparatus of constitutionalism imposing restraints on the prerogatives of monarchy stretching back beyond legal memory, to the pledge of King Canute to govern by the Anglo-Saxon customs of Edgar, the promise of William the Conqueror to continue the laws of Edward the Confessor, the coronation charter of Henry I, and, most notably, the several versions of Magna Carta. It was popular knowledge in the eighteenth century that Charles I, the ruler who had granted some of the early colonial charters, had been executed for violating his compact with the English and Scottish nations. "There is," he was told on being sentenced to death, "a contract and a bargain made between the King and his people, and your oath is taken: and certainly, Sir, the bond is reciprocal." The contract that had been invoked against the father was later breached by the son. Although as a matter of precise law James II had been accused of abandoning the throne, in the popular mind of the eighteenth century he had been disposed for breaking the original contract. The king, in the words of the Massachusetts House of Representatives, not only violated "the original contract with his three kingdoms," he "broke the original contract of the settlement and government of these colonies."[33]

James II's violation of the compact was the last that the crown would be able to commit. During the Glorious Revolution that drove him from the thrones of England, Scotland, and Ireland, the English Parliament changed that country's constitution by seizing supremacy over the monarchy. The constitutional issue resulting from the Glorious Revolution that would be raised by the American Revolution was whether Parliament's *supremacy* over the throne also meant *sovereignty* over the law and constitution. American whigs said it did not and, contending that Parliament stood in the place that the king had constitutionally occupied before the Glorious Revolution, continued to rely upon the protection of contractarian rights much as earlier generations had relied on them in their opposition to Charles I and James II. A point that must be kept in mind when the constitutional arguments are summarized in the following chapters is that, as understood in the mother country and for many Britons, if not most, the original contract remained viable constitutional law despite the Glorious Revolution. This constitutional archaism was illustrated by the marquis of Rockingham's protest against Parliament's attempts to bind some of the colonies by punitive legislation. He had hoped to locate the constitutional limits of Parliament's authority in either the doctrine of consent or the doctrine of contract. "I don't love to claim a right on the foundation of the supreme power of the legislature over all the dominions of the Crown of Great Britain," Rockingham explained. Instead he looked for American acquiescence in "an original *tacit compact*." Unable to find it, he refused to vote to violate the contract that he thought existed.[34]

The contract to which Rockingham referred was not the original contract between the rulers of England and the English people. It was a different, more recent original contract, one made between the rulers of England or Great Britain and the settlers of the American colonies. This can be called the second original contract, the colonial original contract, or the American original contract. The historical event upon which the contractarian doctrine was based was the departure of seventeenth-century English people from the mother country and their emigration to North America. Those first settlers, a governor of Rhode Island explained in 1765, "removed on a firm reliance of a solemn compact and royal promise and grant that they and their successors forever should be free, should be partakers and sharers in all the privileges and advantages of the then English, now British constitution." The legal theory as explained by a London magazine was pure implied contract: "Before their [the first settlers in the colonies] departure, the terms of their freedom, and the relation they should stand in to the mother country, in their emigrant state were fully settled, they were to remain subject to the king, and dependant on the kingdom of *Great Britain*. In return they were to receive protection, and enjoy all the rights and privileges of freeborn *Englishmen*."[35]

There were two elements providing validity to the second original contract: the right of the king to make an agreement and the reliance or expectations of the settlers. The first had to do with whether the king could bind the nation; the second—settlers' reliance or expectations—is what lawyers call "consideration," the price paid by the promisee to make the promise legally binding on the promisor. As the *New York Journal* explained, having been "invested with authority by the whole nation, which gave a sanction to his action," the king "made a contract with the colonists, on the faith of which they trusted the lives and fortunes of themselves and their posterity." Although the contract was implied, the eighteenth-century legal mind was so attuned to contractarian theory that the terms were often explained as mutual promises exchanged between monarch and subjects. For example, consider how, in 1765, the *Boston Evening-Post* worded the contract: "That if the adventurers will hazard their lives and properties in acquiring, according to the rules of justice, possessions in the desert regions of America . . . they shall lose no part of their natural *rights, liberty and property*, by such removal; but that they, *and all their posterity for ever, shall as fully and freely enjoy them, to all intents, constructions, and purposes, as if they and every of them were born in England*."[36]

Once more we are encountering what was the constitutional norm for American whigs: a legal argument that did not originate with them. Just as the original contract had come straight out of English and Irish constitutional history, pleaded by soldiers who fought Charles I and by the descendants of early colonizers who settled Ireland on behalf of Queen Elizabeth, so also did the second original contract. It may look peculiarly designed for the American constitutional problem of the 1770s, but it was not. The Irish had been arguing the second original contract for decades. In 1775, at a time when all attention was focused on what Americans were doing with the second original contract, a pamphlet was printed in Dublin reminding readers that the first English emigrants to Ireland had made a compact with the crown retaining their civil rights under the English constitution. The second original contract was not even a new argument in North America. To cite just one instance, it had been pleaded in the colonies following the New England rebellion of 1689 against the prerogative taxation imposed by Governor Edmund Andros. John Palmer, the most competent common lawyer in Andros's administration, defended prerogative taxes on grounds that North America was conquered territory and, therefore, constitutionally subject to prerogative decrees. Edward Rawson, answering Palmer, denied the fact of conquest, and countered with the second original contract, stating it in terms close to those asserted by American whigs eighty years later: "[T]he King promising [the first New England settlers], if they at their own cost and charge would subdue a Wilderness, and enlarge his Dominions, they and their Posterity after them should enjoy such Priviledges as are in their Charters expressed, of that of not having Taxes imposed on them without their own consent was one."[37]

When reading the following chapters discussing how these several legal theories shaped the constitutional debate leading to the American Revolution it may appear, on first impression, that the controversy was dominated by the original contract and the second original contract. Contractarian theory certainly was appealed to more than any other jurisprudential doctrine, especially on the issue of Parliament's authority to bind the colonies by legislation in all cases whatsoever. What must be noticed, however, is how much the principle of custom was involved in every aspect of the American whig case.

Custom was more than an authority proving rights to constitutionalism. Custom also provided the evidence for that constitutionalism. It was one thing for whigs to contend that the first settlers to the colonies had contracted with Charles I on leaving England. All that claim did was allege the second original contract; it said nothing explicit about the contract's terms. The various stipulations of the contract also had to be established and that was done primarily through the evidence of custom. The contract, remember, was about how future generations of Americans would be governed. The provisions of the contract, therefore, were found by looking at how contemporary colonists and their predecessors had been governed—by looking, that is, at custom as well as at how colonial government currently functioned. The same was true for the authority of purchase and the authority of ownership. There was no better evidence than custom to show what privileges had been purchased and what rights were owned.

Most fundamental of all was the dichotomy of the two constitutions. There was no other aspect of the revolutionary constitutional controversy so calculated to keep apart the two sides. Yet it was an issue never acknowledged by any of the participants. Lawyers and others for both the imperial sovereignty and the American resistance talked to each other as if the distinction between the constitution of legislative command and the constitution of customary rights did not exist. We should not be surprised. Even government officials and legal scholars in the eighteenth century were unlikely to view Parliament in terms of exercising legislative power. True, lawyers would sometimes speak of Parliament as sovereign but in those days Parliament passed so few statutes and issued so few commands that it was hard for anyone to think of it standing in the constitutional place once occupied by Henry VIII and Charles I. People still thought of Parliament in terms of its historical role, as the constitutional check on prerogative power, instituted more to impeach crown officials and receive petitions than to legislate. Both houses of Parliament were so splintered politically during the eighteenth century that almost the only direction Parliament received came from crown manipulation by indirect influence, exercising patronage, pensions, and corruption. Even so, it is puzzling why more attention was not paid to the two constitutions. Perhaps legal thought was just too static to theorize such dramatic change. After all, lawyers on both sides of the Atlantic did not seem to realize that they no longer shared the same notions about what everyone thought the most basic element in English constitutionalism: the rule of law.

The rule of law: If the dichotomy between the two constitutions had a prey during the era of the American Revolution it was the concept of the rule of law. The rule of law was slowly being altered by the emergence of the constitution of sovereign command. In the second half of the eighteenth century, rule of law was not as easily defined as it had been just a few decades earlier. It meant one thing in North America and had for much of the century been assuming a quite different definition in Great Britain. In Great Britain its scope and theory was narrowing from what it had been—or what its exponents had tried to make it mean—in Stuart times. Put in historical perspective, the definition of the rule of law in Great Britain had been changing from what it means in the twentieth-century United States to what it would mean in nineteenth-century Great Britain. Put in terms of eighteenth-century common-law jurisprudence, the concept of the rule of law in Great Britain was coming to mean adherence to the command of the legislature and ceasing to mean adherence to "right" over "power."[38]

As an ideal, the concept of the rule of law in eighteenth-century Great Britain was a support for liberty as liberty was then defined—as a restraint on governmental power, especially arbitrary power, and less as we think of liberty, as liberating the individual from government's restraints. One fundamental element of liberty was the certainty of law, and the certainty of law was established, in part, by the rule of law. "Free Government is the protecting the People in their Liberties by stated Rules," Thomas Gordon had pointed out earlier in the century. "Only the Checks put upon Magistrates make Nations free," his colleague John Trenchard agreed, "and only the want of such Checks makes them Slaves." In the American colonies the concept was summed up by the Connecticut clergyman Jared Eliot. "Blessed be God. . . . We live under a Legal Government," he said, explaining that by "Legal" he meant "Limited." "It is a Corner-Stone of our Political Building, *That no mans Life, Limb, Name, or Estate, shall be taken away but by his Peers and by the known Laws of the Land.*" What distinguished "Law and Freedom from Violence and Slavery," Edmund Burke added, "is, that the property vested in the Subject by a known Law—and forfeited by no delinquency defined by a known [law] could [not] be taken away from him by any power or authority whatsoever."[39]

At its strongest, the rule of law was a general principle that government and governed alike are subject to due process. In popular expression, the concept of the rule of law defined government as "The empire of laws, and not of men," or the circumscribing of power by "some settled Rule or Order of Operation." In the seventeenth century the ideal of the rule of law had obtained constitutional primacy because it circumscribed monarchy. "[I]t is one of the Fundamentals of Law," the prosecutor of Charles I had asserted, "that the King is not above the Law, but the Law [is] above the King." Charles could be criminally charged because a prince disobeying the law was a "rebel." "King Charles," an eighteenth-century writer explained, "either could not, or would not distinguish between the executive power, which our constitution has lodged in the crown, and the supreme power, which our constitution hath lodged in the law of the land, and no where else." When these words were written in 1771, "law of the land" may have meant something quite different in Great Britain than in the colonies. It was unlikely that a majority of Britons at that time thought of "law of the land" or "rule of law" as expressing fundamental, or immutable law, rather than merely changeable positive law. The crown might still be subject to the rule of law, but in Great Britain "law" in this sense was coming to mean what Parliament declared. It was that change of the concept of "law"—whether we call it fundamental, immutable, or constitutional—that American whigs resisted.[40]

Although theory was changing and it is difficult to tell just when certain principles became dominant, in light of the dichotomy of the two constitutions it seems safe to assert that, by the age of the American Revolution in Great Britain, the rule of law no longer included the notion of the sovereignty of law over the ruler. It may even be that the rule of law had become procedural only, not substantive, holding that government actions must conform to legislative command, and that command could be changed at legislative will and pleasure. In other words, the rule of law now restrained power from violating liberty largely by limiting the definition of liberty to the legislatively permitted. "An *English* individual," a writer who thought American resistance in 1775 was legal explained, "cannot, by the supreme authority, be deprived of liberty, unless by virtue of some law, which his representative has had a part in framing." The word "law" in this context had shrunk from meaning "right," as it would have under the constitution of prescriptive, customary rights, to meaning "statute." It was not enough that laws be promulgated and certain for the rule of law to serve the liberty of the individual. "To assert an absolute exemption from imprisonment in all cases," Sir William Blackstone protested, "is inconsistent with every idea of law . . . : but the glory of the English law consists in clearly defining the times, the causes, and the extent, wherefore, and to what degree, the imprisonment of the subject may be lawful."[41]

As understood in Great Britain, therefore, the principle of the rule of law may not have restrained parliamentary power so much as guided it. Certainty of procedure was perhaps its most basic and universally recognized element, and meant, in John Locke's words, "to govern by *promulgated establish'd Laws*, not to be varied in particular Cases." Almost as well known, although in eighteenth-century Great Britain as likely to be breached as to be honored, were the elements that punishment should not be *ex post facto* and property should not be taken without compensation. Another aspect of the rule of law was protection of legal rights. "[T]he very Essence of Government," as an anonymous commentator on revolutionary principles pointed out, "consists in making and executing Stated Rules, for the determining of all Civil Differences, and in doing all other Acts that tend to secure the Subjects against all Enemies Foreign and Domestick, in the quiet Possession of their legal Rights." The most salient expression of the rule of law in eighteenth-century Great Britain, however, the one that American whigs most likely thought of first when asked if Great Britain was ruled by the rule of law, was the principle of equal application. "Laws, in a free State," it was said, should be equally applied. "[T]he Peer should possess no privilege destructive to the Commoner; the Layman obtain no Favour which is denied the Priest; nor the Necessitous excluded from the Justice which is granted to the Wealthy," or, in the words of Locke, there was but "one Rule for Rich and Poor, for the Favourite at Court, and the Country Man at Plough."[42]

In the American colonies the concept of the rule of law was closer to the constitutional values of seventeenth-century England than to the newer constitutional understanding of eighteenth-century Great Britain. For Americans, the rule of law primarily meant to be free of arbitrary power. To understand what colonial whigs meant by the rule of law, therefore, it is necessary to define what they (and eighteenth-century British) meant by arbitrary power, and to do so we must rid ourselves of twentieth-century thoughts about arbitrariness having something to do with despotism, tyranny, or cruel government. It may be today, but that was not the legal definition in the eighteenth century. Then it was not the harshness, the brutality, or the certainty of the exercise of power that made government arbitrary. It was, rather, the possession of power unchecked. Tyrannical power was abuse of power; arbitrary power was power without restraint.

In eighteenth-century parlance on both sides of the Atlantic, arbitrary was the difference between liberty and slavery, right and power, constitutional and unconstitutional. To the eighteenth-century American legal mind, knowing what was arbitrary delineated the concept of the rule of law. "For it is certain," Jared Eliot reminded members of the Connecticut Assembly in 1738, "*That to the Constitution of every Government Absolute Sovereignty must lodge somewhere.* So that according to this Maxim, Every Government must be Arbitrary and Despotick. The difference seems to be here; Arbitrary Despotick Government is, When this Sovereign Power is directed by the Passions, Ignorance & Lust of them that Rule. And a Legal Government, is, When this Arbitrary & Sovereign Power puts it self under Restraints, and lays it self under Limitations." It was, Viscount Bolingbroke had said, a matter of power and not of the type and structure of government. Whether power was vested in a single monarch, in "*the principal Persons of the Community*, or in the *whole Body of the People*," was immaterial. What matters is whether power is without control. "Such Governments are Governments of *Arbitrary Will*," he concluded.[43]

Just as the eighteenth-century concept of arbitrariness should not be confused with cruelness or terror, for it could be benevolent, mild and materially beneficial, so it should not be confounded with absoluteness. "[E]ven *absolute Power*," Locke pointed out, "where it is necessary, is *not Arbitrary* by being absolute, but is still limited by that reason, and confined to these ends, which required it in some Cases to be absolute," such as martial discipline which vests an army officer with power to order a trooper to die but cannot "command that Soldier to give him one penny of his

Money." Law was the distinction. If the officer acted within the parameters of the law, his absolute orders were not arbitrary. That element—law or the rule of law—was all important to eighteenth-century constitutional thought. For "court whigs," Reed Browning has pointed out—and also, it should be added, for most educated Britons and Americans—there were "but two types of government: arbitrary and lawful," or, as John Arbuthnot explained in 1733, "what is not legal is arbitrary."[44]

For the British in the age of the American Revolution this meaning of "legal" had changed as the constitutional principle emerged that Parliament could not be arbitrary in law. English constitutional history, especially the history of the Glorious Revolution, taught Britons that Parliament was the institutionalization of liberty, and, as a consequence, law that was the command of Parliament was the law of liberty. The Glorious Revolution had established the principle of parliamentary supremacy over the crown. Once Parliament attempted to extend that supremacy by claiming parliamentary sovereignty over the law and the constitution, the American theory of the rule of law could not survive in the British constitutional world. The constitutional shock that the Americans would receive when Parliament first attempted to tax the colonies for purpose of revenue had also come to be felt in Great Britain. As late as 1750 there may have been few constitutional theorists in the mother country who imagined that legislative authority could pose a threat to liberty by becoming arbitrary. With the 1760s their numbers increased as the people mistakenly called "radicals" in British politics discovered to their horror that the constitution they thought settled at the Glorious Revolution was fading into obsolescence. A new constitution of arbitrary parliamentary sovereignty was emerging, placing the traditional elements of English (and, therefore, British) liberty in greater jeopardy than had been known even under the Tudors and the Stuarts. It was a constitutional development that American whigs would also be forced to acknowledge, despite great reluctance, within the next decade. No other legal or constitutional consideration contributed more to the coming of the American Revolution than the realization that, in the years since the reign of Queen Anne, the doctrine of parliamentary supremacy was evolving into parliamentary sovereignty, making the House of Lords and the House of Commons not only supreme over the crown, but potentially sovereign over the people, the constitution, and, most extreme of all, over the rule of law. The fact that the concept of the rule of law, for so long understood to be a barrier constraining the power of the crown on behalf of liberty, would not be extended to constrain parliamentary power, sums up much of the American Revolution's constitutional controversy.

Although the clash of the two constitutions cannot be exaggerated, the dichotomy must not be accorded more weight than is its due. The fact that

Great Britain was looking forward to the nineteenth-century constitution of sovereign command while the American colonies were looking back to the seventeenth-century constitution of customary rights may, on first thought, cause the constitutional controversy of the American Revolution to appear to have been a conflict over constitutional modernization. Perhaps the British were modernizing. Better to think of the Americans struggling to preserve the rule of law.

CHAPTER TWO

THE AUTHORITY TO TAX

The British Parliament made two constitutional mistakes during the 1760s. First, it assumed unilaterally that it possessed authority to enact legislation of a type it had never before enacted. That is, Parliament assumed that its authority was derived from the constitution of sovereign command and that it was not restrained by the constitution of customary rights. Parliament's second mistake followed from the first. It assumed constitutional authority to tax the North American colonies for purposes of revenue.

The American Revolution was precipitated by the passage of the Stamp Act of 1765, which imposed a tax on the British colonies in the Caribbean and on the North American mainland. The law required the colonists to purchase stamps to be affixed to every newspaper, legal document, and some other forms of paper sold or distributed in the colonies. Revenue was needed, the British ministry contended, to support British troops stationed in North America.[1] More importantly, it was hoped the income would relieve British taxpayers of the crushing debt that had been accumulated from the recent Seven Years War against France and Spain.

The Stamp Act gave Americans the greatest constitutional shock of their colonial experience; it may have triggered the greatest constitutional shock in all American history. Until 1765, the colonists had been confident Parliament could not tax them for purposes of raising revenue. They thought themselves shielded by the constitution of customary rights and its various maxims of restraint upon legislative power, such as the principle that English people could be taxed only by their own consent or the consent of their representatives. Today their faith in that constitution seems incredible. We read their words—there are certainly enough of them, for they were always boasting of their rights—yet it is hard to believe how completely they basked in its security and gloried in the fact that it made them the freest people in the world.[2] The colonists knew that they, like their fellow Britons living in the mother country, were the envy of Europe. When Parliament promulgated the Stamp Act not only their sense of constitutional security but their confident place in the world came crashing down around them.

The shock spread beyond just American whigs, those people who would rebel against Great Britain in 1776. Also opposing the Stamp Act were those other Americans who would later remain loyalists and support their king if not the Parliament. Just about every educated North American reacted to the perceived constitutional peril posed by the Stamp Act. The word on everyone's lips was "unconstitutional" and the principle informing people that the stamp tax was unconstitutional was precedent. The Stamp Act, Americans said, was unprecedented.

Americans did not assert that the Stamp Act was unprecedented because they had never been taxed by Parliament. It was not the taxation element of the Stamp Act that made it unprecedented. Ever since the Commonwealth period, when Oliver Cromwell and the Puritans had ruled England, Parliament had been imposing taxes on the colonies in the form of import duties. These taxes were constitutional, Americans said, because of the purpose for which they had been enacted. They were taxes imposed to regulate trade, an end made constitutional by custom[3] and by the passage of immemorial time.[4] The Stamp Act's purpose was different. It was to raise revenue from the American colonies, revenue intended for the British treasury.

The colonists were probably right, but as with every question involving custom there were exceptions to the rule casting doubts on the application of the principle. British imperialists, to be sure, would never cotton to the trade-regulation distinction. For them the precedential element was in the tax, not the purpose. All import duties were precedents for the Stamp Act, even legislation clearly stating that the tax was imposed for the purpose of regulation.[5] Here we encounter one of those uncluttered questions of law that Americans would take to the judiciary for solution after 1789 but which, under the British constitution then and now, could not be resolved except by Parliament, a tribunal hardly acceptable to American whigs. Besides, American whigs had no doubts about the constitutionality of the distinction, raising it at the very beginning of the controversy and making it, at the very end, a central prop of the constitutional formula for resolving the crisis

proposed by the Continental Congress and by every colonial assembly. Today it is not possible to determine whether the distinction was constitutionally valid. The reason is that the British side never joined the issue and
hardly debated the distinction. True, some government spokesmen such as
William Knox gave it detailed attention and rejected unconditionally any
thought that there was a constitutional difference between trade imposts
and internal taxes for revenue. Most imperialists, however, did not come to
grips with the distinction, ignoring it rather than trying to answer it on the
legal merits. It may be they did not appreciate the distinction's importance
to colonial whigs, but it is unlikely they did not understand it as it had been
argued before in English constitutional history.[6] Many imperialist commentators confused the distinction with another championed by William Pitt,
the great statesman of that epoch. For reasons of constitutional law[7] Pitt
insisted that there was a fundamental constitutional distinction between
taxation and legislation. Because of that fundamental constitutional distinction, Parliament was incompetent to tax the colonies although sovereign in
all matters of legislation. It was a distinction Pitt defended in speech after
speech[8] but it was rejected by just about everyone else, especially Americans whigs. Imperialists tended to confuse Pitt's taxation-legislation distinction with America's taxation-regulation distinction, thinking that when rejecting the first they rejected the second. Whatever the reason, proponents
of Parliament's authority to tax for revenue cited taxes of trade regulation as
precedents for the Stamp Act as if the Americans had never argued the
distinction. Even so, they did not rest on these precedents alone but made a
strenuous effort to find precedents proving that before 1765 Parliament had
taxed the colonies *for purposes of revenue.*

There were several precedents of taxation for purposes of revenue that had
nothing to do with the regulation of trade. Some of these were as old as the
reign of Charles II and were frequently cited to prove Parliament's constitutional right to tax the colonies for revenue,[9] but on the whole it was generally
admitted only two were of merit, one weak, the other persuasive. The first was
the Greenwich Hospital Act, a tax of sixpence a month on British seamen for
their own support should they became disabled. The British said it had been
collected in the colonies, and that fact made it a precedent. Americans whigs
demurred on both law and facts. The law argument was obvious: that the
Greenwich Hospital assessment, although a tax, was for a limited purpose, not
to raise general revenue. The factual argument that the Greenwich law was
not a precedent was three fold: 1) it had not been collected in the colonies
until the 1760s; 2) even when collected it had been paid under protest; and
3) the tax had been paid only by mariners on merchant ships, not by colonial
fishermen, letting Americans say that if it was a precedent it belonged in the
category of trade regulation, not taxation.[10]

The persuasive precedent was the Post Office Act. The British postal service had a monopoly over the mails in the colonies and the fees collected for carrying letters became part of the public revenue. That fact was important as it made the Post Office, under the premises of the constitution of customary rights, the one, clear precedent supporting the constitutionality of the Stamp Act. Americans distinguished it by contending, as did colonial postmaster Benjamin Franklin when testifying before the House of Commons, that it was not a tax but a fee paid for "regulation and conveniency." Today, this contention seems as persuasive as the British evidence that the Post Office Act was the precedent for an internal tax collected in the colonies for purpose of revenue. Yet Americans did not think their case convincing. The Post Office precedent worried them. We should puzzle over their concern. No other evidence so starkly demonstrates how we no longer share or even understand the constitutional anxieties of the eighteenth century. American whigs were so bothered by the Post Office precedent that in every colony they tried to neutralize if not nullify it altogether. To check the "certainly unconstitutional" imperial post office, they set up a rival system, "a post-office upon constitutional principles" or "what is called a constitutional Post-Office." Again it is worth reflecting how striking this event is from our perspective. Fear of the post-office precedent was so great American whigs not only shunned the British mails, they started a *constitutional* postal service of their own. It was a more drastic step than we might think. The colonists had to know they were saying something positive about the precedent. Because the former post office had been created by Parliament, Boston's committee of correspondence explained, the revenue it raised was "as obnoxious as any other revenue Act." Saying that practically admitted the Post Office Act was a precedent for Parliament's authority to tax for revenue.[11]

The story of the "constitutional" post office is not in all the books on the American Revolution. Many of our twentieth-century writers cannot credit that ideas and doctrine could motivate action. When the "constitutional" post office is mentioned, it is generally explained by twentieth-century values. It has, for example, been argued that the new post office "was much less an attempt to resist a revenue producing act of Parliament than it was part of the committee's over-all effort to see a reliable union established among the colonies." That is not what eighteenth-century American whigs said. "[T]he Cause of American freedom is deeply concerned" in the post-office precedent, a New Yorker explained. It was, he added, a precedent "upon which every other unconstitutional Act has been grounded." That was a strong statement but nowhere near as strong as what the New Yorker said next. If the colonies had their own postal system "it will put an entire Stop to their [the British] laying any further unconstitutional Burdens upon us." We may doubt if his law was correct, but his claim does tell us how much respect some American whigs had for the authority of precedents. As the *Boston Evening-Post* observed when urging people to subscribe to the constitutional post office, it had "the capital design of annihilating that fatal precedent against us—the POST-OFFICE." The Post Office Act was a precedent, perhaps the only precedent for parliamentary taxation upon the colonies for purpose of revenue, and colonial whigs had to counteract it.[12]

Although no one today, not even a common lawyer, would have known what was going on, the tactic of creating a "constitutional" post office was not unique. It was, in fact, a variation on constitutional strategy frequently practiced by American whigs—the strategy of constitutional avoidance.[13]

The constitutional process of avoidance was not something for leaders alone but could be practiced by everyone: the private citizen pledging not to buy taxed tea as part of a nonimportation agreement and even members of the mobs on the street, as American whigs demonstrated at the very onset of the revolutionary controversy. No sooner was the Stamp Act promulgated than colonial crowds began to harass selected imperial officials to prevent its operation. As a general rule the Stamp-Act riots were designed and executed to avoid a precedent of payment. That fact was delineated when the governor of North Carolina, seeking to prevent mob action, "offered to pay himself the whole Duty arising on any Instruments executed on Stampt Paper, on which he should have any Perquisite or Fee; such as Warrants and Patents for Land." Local whigs leaders said no. "[T]he Submission," they contended, "to any Part of so oppressive and (as we think) so unconstitutional Attempts [at parliamentary taxation for revenue], is opening a direct Inlet for Slavery, which all Mankind will endeavour to avoid." In other words, even stamps purchased by the governor would have contributed a precedent for Parliament's authority to tax the colonists for purpose of revenue. Submission to any part of the Stamp Act, the North Carolinians told the governor, "would put it out of our Power to refuse, with any Propriety, a Submission to the whole."[14]

We should underline the exact words of those North Carolina whigs. They were not meant for us but for their contemporaries, people they knew understood the constitutional principle. It is people of later generations who need to be told why enforcement of the Stamp Act "would put it out of our Power" to contest its validity. That was the functional strength of precedent in the eighteenth century. Even more revealing are the constitutional apprehensions felt and the type of avoidance practiced. In North Carolina and every other mainland colony, the whig crowds did not strike out at random imperial officials. Their targets were the agents appointed to distribute the stamps. They "persuaded" all the stamp officials to resign their commissions, and, by making certain there was no one to sell stamps, saw to it there was no precedent of an American taxed by Parliament for purpose of revenue.[15]

The strategy of avoidance worked so well that the ministry repealed the Stamp Act in less than a year. During the remaining decade before the Declaration of Independence, Parliament imposed on the colonies only two other taxes for purpose of revenue. The first, the so-called Townshend duties of 1767, were levied on four products—glass, painters' colors, paper, and tea—imported into North America from Great Britain.[16] Expectations were expressed in Parliament that American whigs, trapped by their own constitutional theory, would not be able to deny that the duties were constitutional. After all, during the Stamp Act debates they had said that "external" taxes imposed on imports were constitutional. But the British understood what they wanted to understand, and, like the progressive historians earlier this century,[17] got the American argument wrong. Colonial whigs had not said the Stamp Act was unconstitutional because it was a direct, "internal" tax, implying that "external" taxes or import duties were constitutional. They objected to the Stamp Act because it was a revenue measure without constitutional precedent. And because the Townshend duties were exactly the same—a revenue measure—colonial whigs opposed the second tax as they had the first, although due to the nature of the levy—there were no agents to harass—their strategy of avoidance had to be different; they boycotted British products.[18]

The Townshend duties were like the Stamp Act in another way. They were a failure. So little income was generated they never became a precedent for Parliament's authority to raise revenue in the colonies. Parliament repealed all of the duties except the one on tea which it later upgraded by converting it into the famous Tea Act of 1773. It is important to understand precisely what Parliament was up to. Like whig mobs against the Stamp Act it was executing constitutional strategy. The Townshend duty on tea had been retained not because the ministry expected revenue but, in the language of the times, to keep up the "right": to maintain Parliament's claim of authority to tax, and to deny American whigs the precedent they would have had had all the Townshend duties been repealed.[19]

These three statutes, the Stamp Act, the Townshend duties, and the Tea Act, are the only tax legislation we need keep in mind. They contain all the taxation aspects of the constitutional controversy leading to the American Revolution. There is, in addition, one important constitutional fact to note. The attempts to tax the colonies for purpose of revenue were decreed by Parliament, not by King George III. All British and American officials and legislators, tories as well as whigs, monarchists as well as republicans, lawyers as well as George III himself, supported the constitutional maxim that the crown could not, on its own authority, impose taxes upon the colonies. There was no British constitutional principle more sacrosanct than that the monarchy could not raise funds independently of either the British or Irish parliaments.

Looking back across two hundred years one might think that if Parliament's supremacy over the crown was so indisputable its supremacy over the constitution should have been as well; that the constitution of sovereign command was "law," and disobedience to what Parliament—the sovereign—commanded put the recalcitrant outside the law. In other words, if Parliament were sovereign under the constitution of sovereign command there could be no ground for constitutional challenge. That is how some accounts of the American Revoultion have been written: that the constitution of sovereign command was the only British constitution and when American whigs arose in opposition to commands such as the Stamp Act they were not acting on constitutional principles but were moved by nonconstitutional factors such as nationalistic yearnings or economic interests.

It is remarkable, but the very first event of the revolutionary controversy—the debate that occurred in the British House of Commons when the government's leader, George Grenville, announced that he would introduce legislation laying for the first time a direct tax for purpose of revenue on the colonies—gave evidence that the constitution of customary right was yet a viable constitution in Great Britain as well as in North America. It is a telling commentary on the constitutional learning of the day that opposition members immediately protested that the proposed Stamp Bill would violate the customary constitutional right of Americans to be taxed for revenue only by their own representative assemblies. It is even more telling that the ministry came to the debate anticipating the constitutional argument against Parliament's authority to tax the colonies for revenue and was prepared to refute it with precedents of taxation without representation; it even carried onto the floor of the house copies of legislation from the time of Henry VIII granting representation to certain counties before taxing them.[20] Most telling of all, a New England newspaper reported, the House of Commons "determined in the Affirmative" that "they [the Commons and the House of Lords] had power to lay such a Tax, on the colonies" even though the people of North America "had no Representative in parliament."[21]

It would be easy to misinterpret what the eighteenth century thought of these events. From the political perspective of the twentieth century we would say that the leaders of Great Britain, at the very beginning of the constitutional controversy, anticipated the constitutional defense that would be raised by American whigs and rejected it. From the constitutional perspective of the eighteenth century, however, these three events—especially adoption by the House of Commons of the resolution asserting Parliament's authority to tax the colonies—indicated that legal arguments about Parliament's authority would not be settled by appeals to the constitution of sovereign command. The controversy would be shaped by the doctrines of the constitution of customary rights: contract, purchase, the right to be taxed only by constitutional consent, and custom.

The constitutional debate about taxes could almost be told by contract theory alone. In all of American history there is not a more extensive instance of contractarian constitutional jurisprudence. At least five different contracts were argued supporting either the colonial whig or British imperialist side. They were: 1) the original contract made in the hidden mists of an immemorial past between the earliest kings of England and the English people, a contract Americans thought still binding in eighteenth-century Great Britain as well as in North America; two versions of the second original contract, one, 2) the colonial original contract between the Stuart kings of England and the first settlers of the colonies extending the rights and procedures of the original contract to North America; the other, 3) the settlement contract, creating an exception to the constitutional right of consent to taxation by stipulating Parliament could tax in return for bearing the costs of settlement; 4) the imperial contract stipulating that Americans, in consideration for Great Britain's military protection, contribute financially to imperial defense by paying parliamentary taxes to the British treasury; and 5) the commercial contract, in answer to or in novation of the imperial contract, stipulating that Great Britain exercised a monopoly over and enjoyed the profits of the colonial trade in lieu of receiving any further compensation for providing imperial defense.

There is a theoretical fact of law laid starkly bare by the amazing emphasis on contract. It is the derivative nature of eighteenth-century constitutionalism. Constitutionalists of that day were not inclined to seek authority for doctrine in universal deductions or moral arguments. They sought constitutional principle in positive, practical experience, even when, as with the various versions of the original contract, the promise and consideration were implied from supposed events. As Reverend Jonathan Lee said when delivering Connecticut's 1766 election sermon, "Dominion, or right to rule, is evidently founded neither in nature or grace, but compact, and consideration." Contractarian authority was especially pertinent for the colonies, Governor Stephen Hopkins of Rhode Island explained, because the first settlers "came out from a kingdom renowned for liberty, from a constitution founded on compact." Much followed from that fact including the ease and versatility with which the language of common-law contract slipped into the constitutional debates. In fact, the vocabulary of contract may be implicit evidence that the participants understood they were dealing with a crisis more constitutional than political, one that could be solved if a satisfactory contractarian formula were found. The object, a London magazine claimed in 1774, was "to establish a form of government, a compact, between Great-

Britain and its Colonies, wherein the power of the former, and the liberties of the latter, shall be fairly and clearly ascertained."[22]

American whigs made their most valiant attempt at defining that compact when trying to resolve the taxation crisis. They did so chiefly by reformulating various versions of the original contract. Due to the constitutional question posed by parliamentary taxation of the colonies, the English original contract, although in constitutional theory the most important of the five contracts that were argued, did not figure prominently in the debate. Our concern is with the second original contract which metastasized from the English original contract the provision that taxes could be levied only with the consent of those taxed. It was easy to assume that the first settlers would have insisted that the most vital guarantee of English liberty should be incorporated into the second original contract. Of course, those first settlers would have known that the "principal privilege implied" in the "original contract," as the Massachusetts House explained, "is freedom from all taxes, but such as they shall consent to in person, or by representatives of their free choice and election." The exact terms they negotiated were confidently stated by the Virginia House of Burgesses: it was "their ancient and inestimable Right of being governed by such Laws respecting their internal Polity and Taxation as are derived from their own Consent."[23]

The Burgesses mentioned another stipulation of the second original contract when also claiming that the right of consenting to taxes had been "ever quietly possessed" by Americans "since first by Royal Permission and Encouragement they left the Mother Kingdom to extend its Commerce and Dominion."[24] Part of the consideration the first settlers had paid the king in return for his promise that the right to taxation by consent would cross the Atlantic was to extend the commerce and dominion of the mother country. That payment was also the colonists' factual answer to British attempts to formulate a British variation of the second original contract. That imperialist version of the second original contract, what can be called "the settlement contract," theorized that the colonies had been settled at English expense and sustained during their early years by English taxpayers. In the settlement contract the settlers and their descendants are obligated to repay these costs by accepting parliamentary taxation. The settlement contract was premised on several counts—duty, reasonable expectations, gratitude, and justice—but in the most frequently stated and fully developed argument it rested on an implied promise arising out of a benefit conferred.

It is astonishing how much the revolutionary controversy was conducted like a common-law litigation even though there was no tribunal to which the parties could appeal except the court of public opinion. American whigs answered the British version of the second original contract just as they would have had they been in a court of law, by marshalling facts. The facts were most concisely stated by the people of Ipswich, Massachusetts: "when our Fathers left their Native Country . . . they came of their Own accord and at their own Expence and took possession of a country they were obliged to Buy or Fight for and to which the Nation had no more Right than [to] the Moon." Pennsylvania, its House of Representatives asserted, had been settled and expanded "without the least Expense of the Mother State," and Virginia, the people of Fairfax County pointed out, "was not Settled at the National expence of England, but at the private expence of the Adventurers, our Ancestors, by solemn Compact with, and under the auspices and protection of the British Crown."[25]

It is indicative of how seriously American whigs took this aspect of the revolutionary controversy that they expended much time and paper uncovering the evidence needed to muster a factual defense. Even more revealing, they did not rest on facts alone but developed a legal defense as well. To the extent that the British claim of a settlement contract could be analogized to the *quantum meruit* ("as much as it is worth") count in common-law assumpsit, American whigs replied that the *quantum meruit* was canceled by the debt Great Britain owed eighteenth-century colonists for what their seventeenth-century ancestors had done; the settlement contract, they argued, was set off by the settlement debt.[26] It was a debt for which "the Colonists here have paid a valuable Consideration," the Pennsylvania House of Representatives contended, "by planting and improving a Wilderness, far distant from their Mother Country, at a vast Expense, and the Risk of many Lives from the savage Inhabitants, whereby they have greatly increased the Trade and Commerce of the Nation." This time the obligation created by the consideration was not an executory contract but a debt. "It was but a debt due to these brave adventurers, and their immediate descendants that the right of taxation should be vested in people upon the spot," that is the people then living in Pennsylvania and the other colonies.[27]

We might expect that for both sides, Americans as well as Britons, the settlement debt exhausted contractarian jurisprudence. In fact, it did not. The unwritten eighteenth-century constitution was so ambiguous and so tactile that neither the whigs nor the imperialists dared leave an alternative theory unargued. In fact, it was the British imperialists who introduced the contract that, at least in the debate about taxation, was the most frequently discussed. This was the imperial contract, a particularly uncomplicated contract. Americans, by that contract, were obliged to pay taxes imposed by Parliament for purpose of revenue in return for British military protection.

Most writers invoking the imperial contract strove doughtily to formulate a contractual theory of enforceability. One obvious theory was reciprocity. "[T]he first and great principle of all government, is, *that support is due in return for protection*," was probably the maxim most often stated. "*On this acknowledged principle*," it was said, "*the stamp-act was planned*." That claim seems correct; George Grenville, the minister responsible for the Stamp Act, made the argument several times. "Protection and obedience are reciprocal," he told the Commons. "Great Britain protects America; America is bound to yield obedience." By obedience he meant the payment of taxes, and why not? Americans were obliged by reciprocity. "When they want the protection of this kingdom, they are always very ready to ask it. . . . The nation has run itself into an immense debt to give them their protection." It was the constitutional duty of the colonies to contribute a fair share toward the public expense, especially to that part of imperial expense arising from themselves.[28]

A second theory of enforceability was that costs incurred created an obligation to repay. "[N]o man," Samuel Johnson explained, "has a right to security of government without bearing his share of its inconveniences. . . . The payment of fleets and armies may be justly required from those for whose protection fleets and armies are employed." The same liability could be theorized on grounds of request, grant, and acceptance. All one had to do was assume or prove that colonial governments had asked protection, the mother country had provided it, and, as a matter of law, the imperial contract imposed a binding obligation on the colonies.[29]

The strongest theories for enforceability analogized the imperial contract to a common-law obligation, utilizing the benefit-conferred rule of the action of debt, the detriment-suffered test of *indebitatus assumpsit*, or the unjust-enrichment doctrine of quasi-contracts. Either the war Great Britain had just fought against France in defense of the American colonies had been so costly "that those who had reaped the chief Benefit, should contribute a Portion towards defraying the Expence which had attended the Acquisition," or "[t]he advantages the colonies obtained by the peace, and the debt incurred by the late war, undertaken for their defence only, with other considerations too numerous to be mentioned here, required some retribution from them." An argument made in 1776 relied upon both benefit-conferred and detriment-suffered considerations. "We have fought, we have conquered for the Americans. We have restored Peace to their Possessions at Home, and freed them from Apprehensions of Disturbances from Abroad. In so doing we have contracted a Debt too heavy for English Shoulders to bear."[30]

One American answer in law was that the war effort against the French and Indians had not been disproportionately British and that the colonies had contributed their fair share. The contention appears, at first glance, to be an argument of fact, as it was, but just as significantly it was one of law. It was an argument of fact because it reduced the British claim of defending the colonies to a contributing role, denying that the mother country alone

had won the imperial victory. As an argument of law it provided a legal answer to that element of the imperial contract invoking the duty of Americans
to pay for their own defense. The colonies denied the obligation not only on
the grounds that there was no contract, but that they had paid and were
continuing to pay all that legally could be demanded.

American whigs raised a remarkable variety of defenses to the imperial
contract. For example, they argued that the payment stipulated—i.e., the
right of Parliament to impose taxes on the colonies for purposes of raising revenue—was constitutionally exorbitant for the consideration rendered.
Perhaps the "most legal" defense was that, as a matter of law, the contract
was unenforceable. There were two grounds. First, that under the second
original contract between the crown and the first settlers, Great Britain had
assumed a constitutional duty to protect the colonies. That contract took
precedence over and nullified the imperial contract. Second, protection
from the nation to one part of the nation, without a specific promise from
that part, could not impose an obligation. "Put the case," a Massachusetts
lawyer suggested, "that the town of *Portsmouth* or any other seaport had
been besieged and the like sums expended in its defense, could any have
thought that town ought to be charged with the expense?" There was a
uniform answer. "If Britain has protected the property of America, it does
not constitute her the owner of that property. She has, for her own sake,
protected, in their turns, almost every country in Europe, but that does not
make her the proprietor of those countries, or give her a power of taxation
over them."[31]

American defenses of fact disproving the imperial contract are too extensive to be treated in detail. Stripped to their bare essentials they were: the
colonies, especially New England, paid more than their share of the costs of
the Seven Years War; it had been a European war, not an American war,
with France and Britain fighting in North America for European purposes
and to extend their own possessions; and that most of the fruits of victory
had gone to the British, especially the Indian trade, which was primarily a
British enterprise, carried on with British manufactures, for the profit of
British merchants.[32]

It may not have mattered that the factual defense against the imperial
contract was not as convincing as colonial whigs would have liked. The
argument, after all, was forensic, and lack of persuasion need not be conclusive if there was yet a counterargument to be offered. American whigs and
their British supporters, suspecting that they had not clinched their factual
case against the imperial contract, attempted to nullify its implications with
a novation or yet another contract. That contract, the fifth, or what can be
called the commercial contract, was premised on a deceptively simple contention. If Great Britain had, in fact, gone to war to protect the colonies,

she had not done so "out of disinterested regard for them; but to secure the profits of their trade; a trade, which, had they become subjects of *France*, must have been lost to *England*." What had Britain been protecting, a member inquired of the House of Commons in 1775, "yourselves or them?" The trade of the colonies was controlled by the mother country for the profit of the British people. Even if London provided the colonies with protection, the commercial contract asked, what difference did it make? "Have they not paid for it by the benefits of their commerce?"[33]

The various theories upon which the commercial contract was propped are of interest only for showing how technical the legal aspects of the revolutionary controversy became. These included: 1) a benefit conferred—American acquiescence in parliamentary navigation laws that required the colonies purchase only British products and funnel all American trade into the mother country, repaying with the profits of commerce whatever debt was owed for protection under the imperial contract ("By these means, the colonies not only pay for their own protection, but help protect all his Majesty's dominions, in all parts of the world. It is upon this trade to the plantations, that the safety of the whole nation depends, and more particularly of *Great Britain* itself");[34] 2) a detriment suffered—the profits Great Britain made from the commercial contract, William Pitt contended in the House of Commons, not only brought vast profits to Great Britain, but inflicted extensive losses on the colonies, constituting sufficient consideration to repay any debt owed ("This is the price America pays you for her protection");[35] and 3) a subrogate tax—that Britain's monopoly of colonial trade was, as the duke of Grafton told the House of Lords, "in reality a tax," or, as Americans were fond of quoting a former prime minister, Robert Walpole, "the colonists, by the profits of our trade with them, *enabled* us to pay *our* taxes, which was the same as paying taxes to the mother country; and that, by the restrictions, under which we have laid their commerce, all their money comes to the mother-country; and the mother-country can at most have but their all."[36]

Agreeing that the trade monopoly was a tax, imperialist William Knox came to an opposite conclusion from that of Pitt and Walpole. That Parliament customarily taxed the colonies by regulating their commerce, he contended, was not a contract barring parliamentary taxation, but precedent proving the authority of Parliament to tax the colonies for purpose of revenue. Other imperialists said that the detriments were mutual or that even with the monopoly the benefits conferred on the colonies were more substantial than the profits paid to Great Britain. And so the arguments went, back and forth, one side relying on a contract and the other replying that the contract was deficient either in law or in facts. The extensive debate—often involving painstaking study of history, precedents, and commercial statistics—

merits the close attention of every serious student of the American Revolution. It is not necessary to provide more details, however, for the important constitutional lesson has been drawn. It is the extent to which contractarian principles shaped the revolutionary controversy. There is a good deal to be learned by just considering how legal the debate became. That fact tells us much about how English-speaking people in the eighteenth century regarded law and the role that they wanted law to play in governing their lives. American whigs and British imperialists formulated theories such as the settlement contract and the imperial contract because they expected their fellow citizens to be motivated by contractual commitments. They pleaded technical legal doctrine because they not only thought other people would understand but would act on obligations created by benefits conferred, duties arising from promises implied, debts due for detriments suffered, and repayments owed for services rendered. A remarkably high percentage of what later commentators have termed the *political* values of the American whig and the British imperialist belonged to a legal world we have lost.

The energy and thought spent by participants in the revolutionary debate proving and disproving various contracts suggest that some people felt the original contract was constitutionalism's strongest authority. If so, the laity differed from lawyers. For those trained in common law the doctrine of custom was the main foundation of the British constitution. Of course, educated nonlawyers also knew that custom was constitutional authority. Certainly American whigs were as skilled at citing it as were members of London's Inns of Court. Consider the impeccable constitutional doctrine voted by the town meeting of Providence, Rhode Island, at the height of the Stamp Act crisis. Declaring that their "particular Rights as Colonists" were "precisely known and ascertained, by uninterrupted Practice and Usage from the first Settlement of this Country, down to this Time," the people of Providence instructed their representatives to the colonial Assembly to ignore the Stamp Act because Rhode Islanders had, since the colony's founding, "enjoyed the Right of being governed by their own Assembly, in the Article of Taxes." The continuous, uninterrupted enjoyment of that right, as a matter of constitutional law, vested Rhode Island's Assembly with the "exclusive Right to lay Taxes and Imposts upon the Inhabitants of this Colony: and . . . every Attempt to vest such Power in any Person or Persons whatever, other than the General Assembly aforesaid, is unconstitutional, and hath a manifest Tendency to destroy *British*, as well as *American Liberty*."[37]

The Providence resolutions are a textbook application of the doctrine of custom. Custom was the constitutional authority forbidding Parliament to tax the colony for revenue and vesting the Assembly with exclusive jurisdiction: "uninterrupted Practice and Usage" from the beginning of relevant

time, "the first Settlement of this Country." That authority—"that continuous, uninterrupted enjoyment"—was why the Stamp Act was unconstitutional and why the Assembly's right to tax Rhode Islanders was constitutionally exclusive. For Parliament to disregard it could "destroy *British* as
well as *American Liberty*" because parliamentary disdain could weaken the
authority of custom and the authority of custom was the main safeguard
protecting liberty.[38]

Both the doctrine of custom and the evidence that the colonies had
always taxed themselves was so well understood during the era of the American Revolution that appeals to the authority of custom against the constitutionality of the Stamp Act, the Townshend duties, and the tea tax tended to
follow the same formula. The argument has been extensively detailed elsewhere[39] and need not be repeated here, especially as we must return to
custom in the discussion of Parliament's authority to legislate, a more gravid
issue for the doctrine of custom than the authority to tax. Better to sum up
the use made of custom against Parliament's claim of the authority to tax by
quoting one of the most effective pronouncements of the doctrine applied
to the issue of the constitutionality of the Stamp Act. It was drafted by
Connecticut's governor and adopted by the Assembly even before the Stamp
Bill was enacted into law. By Connecticut's original charter, obtained from
King Charles I, it was asserted, "a full power of legislation is granted to the
colony."

> [T]hese powers, rights, and privileges the colony has been in possession
> of for more than a century past. This power of legislation necessarily
> includes in it an authority to impose taxes. . . . These privileges and
> immunities, these powers and authority, the colony claims not only in
> virtue of their right to the general principles of the British constitution
> and by force of the royal declaration and grant in their favor [*i.e.*, the
> second original contract], but also as having been in possession, enjoy-
> ment, and exercise of them for so long a time, and constantly owned,
> acknowledged, and allowed to be just in the claim and use thereof by
> the crown, the ministry, and the Parliament, as may evidently be shown
> by royal instructions, many letters and acts of Parliament, all supposing
> and being predicated upon the colony's having and justly exercising
> these privileges, powers, and authorities, and what better foundation
> for, or greater evidence of, such rights can be demanded or produced is
> certainly difficult to be imagined.[40]

This argument outlines customary constitutionalism at its strongest. Long
usage, exclusive possession, and London's acquiescence proved custom not
only as authority for the Assembly's claim to tax Connecticut's residents but
to make any tax by Parliament unconstitutional. The authority of custom was

reinforced by the second original contract which, in this case, was not implied but was an explicit agreement which had been executed at various times by both crown and Parliament. Everyone coming across this statement during the eighteenth century knew they were reading an argument of law.

The last point is made only because today we might forget what was legal in the eighteenth century. It is worth being reminded of the gulf between legal thought now and legal thought then. Everything, of course, was not different. There were issues raised in the revolutionary debate over Parliament's authority to tax the colonies for revenue that today are readily recognized as legal, even if we no longer think of them as rights. Two, for example, were the right to security and the right to government, rights put in jeopardy by any unconstitutional command from Parliament, whether or not it was a command of taxation.[41] Another right, one more obviously threatened by unconstitutional taxation, was the right to property.[42] A right endangered by the Stamp Act particularly was the right to trial by jury in criminal cases. Prosecutions for violation of the Act—refusal to pay the stamp tax or to use stamped paper as specified by the statute—were not cognizable at common law as constitutional custom dictated, but prosecuted in a vice-admiralty court with both law and fact determined by an imperially-appointed judge applying civil, not common law. Americans thought this a horrendous violation of their inherited, owned constitutional rights and, as much as any other grievance, depredation of the jury right dramatized to people in North America how partial parliamentary legislation could be.[43] The rights to government, security, property, and the jury, helped to make colonists aware of the constitutional issues posed by parliamentary taxation. They were extraordinarily effective as propaganda, but raised few unique legal questions. They can be studied elsewhere,[44] and attention here can concentrate on a constitutional right peculiar to the taxation controversy, the doctrine of consent to taxation.

The doctrine of consent to taxation was the bone and marrow of the revolutionary controversy, involving not only one of the most fundamental principles of English constitutional history, but invoking aspects of all the other maxims of law that were debated, including the original contract, the second original contract, the authority of precedent and analogy, and the binding force of custom.

Consent-to-tax was easily stated. "[I]t is," Pennsylvania's Assembly insisted, "the inherent birthright, and indubitable privilege of every British subject to be taxed only by his own consent, or that of his legal representatives."[45] Numerous British officials as well as students of the constitution in both the mother country and the colonies called consent the most important rule that the constitution of Great Britain had inherited from English con-

stitutionalism.[46] Only a very few denied consent was part of the constitution,[47] although quite a few would have limited its scope, asserting it was
nowhere as broad as American whigs sought to make it. "To say," a pamphleteer explained, "that no Englishman is to be taxed, without his consent,
either in person, or by his representatives, is merely sound without sense,
and not true in fact; but must be limited, by the constitutional mode of
taxation, which only requires, that no Englishman shall be taxed, without
the consent of a representative body of men, in parliament." That was one
meaning of constitutional consent—that the crown could not impose prerogative taxation. British subjects could constitutionally be taxed only by
Parliament. Surprisingly, the argument was not extensively developed. Most
Britons seem to have agreed with the lord mayor, aldermen, and livery of
London when they told the king, "[W]e esteem it an essential, unalterable
principle of liberty, the source and security of all constitutional rights—that
no part of the dominion can be taxed without being represented." They did
not say "without being represented in Parliament," because they meant taxation by representation, not taxation by Parliament.[48]

There is a small point about the consent-to-taxation doctrine that should
be made if for no other reason than that it has often been misunderstood in
the twentieth century. Occasionally an American politician or individual
American citizen is said to complain that they or someone else is being taxed
"without representation," which, it is added, violates the principle for which
Americans fought the Revolution. The contention is not legally accurate.
The colonists did not claim the doctrine of consent to taxation as an American right. It had been a minor aspect of colonial constitutional law before
1765,[49] and it would not be law later under the United States Constitution.
Taxation by consent was a British not an American rule. Few things tell us
more about the legal premises of the revolutionary controversy than the fact
that colonial whigs, when claiming the right to be taxed only by consent,
were not talking about taxation or rates of assessment but about equality
with their fellow subjects in the mother country—that is, the right to be
taxed only by their elected representatives.

There was no other constitutional doctrine argued during the controversy
on which Americans stood on more solid ground. Consent to taxation was
not only one of the best known legal premises in English history, but was
also believed to be one of the oldest—traceable, some experts thought, to
time immemorial, even to the gothic constitution in the Saxon forests on
the continent, when the doctrine was "a fundamental part of all European
constitutions." It was the quintessential constitutional custom, creating a
civil right limiting governmental power. It was also the quintessential stipulation of the English original contract. "The Law of England, whereby the
Subject was exempted from Taxes and Loans, not granted by common

Consent of Parliament," John Pym, speaking on behalf of the Commons, told the Lords, "was not introduc'd by any Statute, or by any Charter or Sanction of Princes, but by the antient and fundamental Law, issuing from the first Frame and Constitution of the Kingdom." Pym spoke in 1628.[50]

The history of Charles I made the precedents of consent the best known precedents in eighteenth-century constitutional law. "Was not," a correspondence of the *New London Gazette* asked in 1765, "the raising taxes by ship money, &c. without the consent of the good people of England who were to pay them, and arbitrary courts of trial, contrary to the rights of Englishmen and the common usages of the land, principal grievances and causes of civil war in the reign of Charles I?" Why, an anonymous London pamphleteer asked eleven years later, had Charles been opposed? "To secure to the People the right of making for themselves those laws by which they were to be governed, and the right of laying that taxation on themselves which they themselves were to pay." "If our ancestors," a second London pamphlet explained, "had not resisted in the days of Charles the First, the constitution of this country would have been subverted, and an unlimited power of arbitrary taxation vested in the prince, on the same principles on which we claim a right to tax America."[51]

The beheading of Charles I ended the threat that prerogative taxation would become constitutional in England. The doctrine of taxation by consent rested, as before, on constitutional custom, custom now made stronger by the defeat of Stuart prerogativism and stated in the legal literature as a constitutional absolute. Consent was generally expressed as a right vested in Parliament but occasionally described, as American whigs described it, as a right protecting property against any arbitrary taking. Andrew Marvell in 1677 anticipated colonial language when he insisted that "No money is to be Levied but by a common consent."[52]

Considering the flexibility of constitutional advocacy, it is not surprising that the taxation-by-consent doctrine derived even more authority from analogy than from precedent. After all, the colonies were contending that they were constitutionally exempted from parliamentary taxes imposed for revenue. Pointing out other divisions of the realm of England or of the British empire which had not been taxed by Parliament was to cite legal authority directly on point. Even better if these jurisdictions never taxed by Parliament had been taxed by their own legislatures.

The best known analogies were drawn from units of local government within the realm, particularly the Palatinate counties of Chester and Durham and the principality of Wales. It may be that no other facts used to prove arguments of law during the revolutionary period were so frequently mentioned, at least during the first two or three years. For many people in the mother country, the controversy had commenced when, in the most memorable exchange of the Stamp Act crisis, William Pitt and George Grenville debated in the House of Commons the meaning of the Chester-Durham analogies. Grenville made the mistake of mentioning them first. Both Chester and Durham, he contended, had been taxed by Parliament before gaining representation in Parliament. Grenville "then quoted the acts, and desired that they might be read"—a remarkable indication not only of how well he was prepared for a constitutional debate, but also the importance of the Palatine analogies in English constitutional history and eighteenth-century British constitutional thought. Just as revealing, Pitt answered Grenville in kind, asserting that the analogies proved the opposite of what Grenville claimed: that Parliament could not tax the colonies. He also reminded the Commons of yet a third analogy, one with which his listeners were so familiar he simply mentioned it, assuming that everyone understood its relevance. "Why did the gentleman confine himself to Chester and Durham?" Pitt asked. "He might have taken a higher example in Wales; Wales, that never was taxed by Parliament, till it was incorporated."[53]

The hundreds of later references of the analogies of Chester and Durham generally reiterated the arguments of Grenville and Pitt. The evidence was considered so important that the preambles of both statutes were printed several times in the British press. There was little debate about what the analogies meant. "It was found," as one writer explained in 1774, "that the people of those districts were taxed and not represented, and the language of the legislature is the same to them all.—If you pay duties and taxes it is your right to be represented, and partake in the choice of those that lay them upon you, and therefore we grant you representatives to all future parliaments." As Pitt said in the debate with Grenville, the analogy of Wales seemed stronger because Wales had not been taxed until it was granted representation. For those who believed Wales got representation in order to be taxed constitutionally, the analogy was even more persuasive.[54]

Stronger in the minds of some lawyers than historical analogies drawn from the past were current analogies—analogies which were functional in the 1760s. These were Guernsey, Jersey, Alderney, Sark, and Ireland, then all taxed by their own assemblies and not by the British Parliament. The four channel islands were especially convincing, a commentator explained, as they "are not taxed by the British parliament at all . . . and I never heard that the British parliament ever offered to hinder them to lay on their own taxes, or to lay on additional ones, when they are not represented."[55]

The Irish analogy was less persuasive. Unlike the four Channel islands which eighteenth-century constitutionalists believed never had been taxed for revenue by Parliament, Ireland had been taxed occasionally. Moreover, Ireland had been conquered by England—several times—which in constitutional law meant that its laws and constitution could be changed by the conqueror at will. American whigs did not want to be analogized to a conquered country and, on the whole, cited Ireland as an object lesson they should avoid, not as an analogy for the right to be taxed only by consent.[56]

In the end the debate over the consent doctrine was resolved less by arguments about contracts, precedent, and analogy than by application of principle. British imperialists did not dispute that the doctrine was good constitutional law—that Americans had a right to be taxed only by their own consent or the consent of their representatives—yet there was a problem of definition. It may come as a surprise, but there were few positive law differences between American and British constitutional law. American constitutional values were British constitutional values because they shared the legacy of a common English patrimony. Practically the only difference between American constitutional practice and British constitutional law was in the definition of representation.

The word describing the American theory was *direct*. It did not matter if a taxpayer was eligible to vote. What mattered was that the taxpayer was resident in a voting district in which most adult males had the right to vote and which elected a representative to the legislative body possessing the authority to tax. That elective representative gave the taxpayer direct representation. By that measure—the measure of a developing American constitutional law—the colonists were not represented in Parliament. No colonial voting district, not even a colony as a whole, elected a single member of the House of Commons. No Americans who were not resident in England, Scotland, Wales, or the Isle of Man, and who owned certain property or lived in specific, designated places, voted in parliamentary elections.

The British word was *virtual*, not direct. The doctrine of virtual representation was not new law invented to deal with the American problem. It was a constitutionalist explanation of how people not qualified to vote, such as women and residents of certain municipalities, were represented and, therefore, taxed by consent. To most British imperialists applying the doctrine to the colonies was a matter of course. "The Parliament of Great Britain virtually represents the whole Kingdom," George Grenville explained to the Commons. "There can be no doubt," Lord Chief Justice Mansfield expanded in the House of Lords, "but that the inhabitants of the colonies are as much represented in parliament as the greatest part of the people of England are represented. . . . A member of parliament chosen for any borough, represents not only the constituents and inhabitants of that particular place, but he represents the inhabitants of every other borough in Great Britain. He represents the city of London, and all other the commons of this land, and the inhabitants of all the colonies and dominions of Great Britain, and is, in duty and conscience, bound to take care of their interests." That was one justification of virtual representation: the universal interests of the representative. A better explanation focused on the constitutional role of the electors rather than the agency of the representative. The members of the Commons, a writer in *Gentleman's Magazine* pointed out, were not chosen by the whole population but elected *"by persons of a particular class only,"* by people entrusted with the vote by constitutional law. It therefore followed that, as "all *British* subjects are legally represented, then he that lives in *Pennsylvania* is, to all intents and purposes, as effectually and legally represented by a parliament so chosen, as he who lives in *London*."[57]

The doctrine was based on the reality of British society, not on American considerations. The great majority of the English, Scots, and Welsh were ineligible to vote. Their ranks included not only such obvious groups as children, the landless, Roman Catholics, and women, but most of the adult male population, among whom were the owners of land held in copyhold tenure, inhabitants of large boroughs such as Leeds, Manchester, Halifax, and Birmingham that had not been accorded the franchise, and other persons whose wealth was held in personal rather than real property. They were all represented virtually, that is, "according to the constitutional customs, usages, and rights of the kingdom."[58]

British constitutionalists said the colonists had "no cause to complain when they are in the same condition as *many* of the natives of G. Britain," that is, "the same situation as the people of those great towns [Birmingham, *et al.*], and all the villages, and open country, which contain thousands, and tens of thousands of people, in Great Britain, who have no power of election." There were, after all, "more millions of subjects unrepresented in England, and yet taxed, than there are inhabitants in British America."[59]

It is sometimes written that the Americans thought virtual representation was not part of the constitution. That is not true. Colonial whigs did not question that virtual representation was constitutional law in Great Britain and that the virtually represented there were constitutionally represented. All they disputed was whether the doctrine could apply constitutionally to them. It contained constitutional safeguards making members of Parliament functionally representative of the nonelectors resident in Great Britain, safeguards that did not work for Americans. These safeguards were the maxim of local interests and local knowledge, the maxim of shared interests, the maxim of shared burdens, and the maxim of equal assessments.

Existing more as theory than practice in eighteenth-century Britain, the maxim of local interests and local knowledge was the least important of the four safeguards. It would be hardly worth mentioning but for the fact that its relevance to North America was so easily refuted. No imperial parliament, Charles James Fox observed, "can legislate with justice and propriety, where the contingencies of locality and interests of individuality cannot be ascertained. Indeed, the greatest principle of legislation, in this instance is lost.—

The representatives themselves having no local attachment for their constituents."[60]

A more significant safeguard for making virtual representation functionally
representative of nonelectors in Great Britain was the maxim of shared
interests. In Parliament there was always some member who shared the
interest of every nonelector and, therefore, represented the interest of at
least some nonelectors. The shared interest might be locality, profession,
land ownership, trade, financial investment, or craft. As long as there was
one member sharing that interest, let us say an army officer, then all army
officers, including those who could not vote, had their interests as army
officers represented. In addition, there were interests everyone shared, such
as their interest in the nation's welfare. "The members of parliament, their
families, their friends, their posterity must be subject, as well as others, to
the laws," the future United States Supreme Court justice, James Wilson,
pointed out. "Their interest, and that of their families, friends, and posterity,
cannot be different from the interest of the rest of the nation. A regard to
the former will, therefore, direct to such measures as must promote the
latter. But is this the case with respect to America?" It was a question that
colonial imperialists were apt to answer one way and colonial whigs in quite
a different way.[61]

The most important constitutional safeguard making members of Parliament representative of the unenfranchised was the maxim of shared burdens. Under the maxim of shared burdens, members of Parliament could
not impose on any part of the population burdens of taxation that the
members did not impose upon themselves. They could not tax nonelectors
as a separate class, and impose upon them more taxes than they imposed
upon themselves and on the electors who had voted for them. If Parliament
authorized a land tax, for example, everyone in Great Britain, except members of the royal family, was liable to pay that tax, including members of
Parliament and electors just as much as nonelectors. It was with this maxim—
that legislators shared the burdens they imposed—that virtual representation most completely broke down when applied to Americans. In Great
Britain, Richard Price explained, "it is impossible that the represented part
should subject the unrepresented part to arbitrary power, without including
themselves. But in the Colonies it is *not* impossible. We know that it *has*
been done." More than that, there was strong incentive for Parliament to do
it. Taxes laid on Americans to enrich the British treasury not only relieved
burdens on the constituents of the members of the House of Commons, it
relieved burdens on the members themselves. "We have experienced," Wilson complained, "what an easy matter it is for a minister with an ordinary
share of art, to persuade the parliament and the people, that taxes laid on
the colonies will ease the burdens of the mother country." The maxim of

shared burdens did not support Parliament's virtual representation over the colonies. It furnished, rather, an argument why, in the matter of taxes, Parliament could never be representative of colonial America. Can anything, a "Freeholder" of Worcester, Massachusetts, asked, "be more terrible than to yield up our lives, and property, to be solely at the arbitrary will of a parliament, which is under no restraint in our favor either of interest or affection; but whose interest and affection are against us?"[62]

As "Freeholder" indicates, American whigs could turn the maxim of shared burdens back on Parliament when opposing general legislation as well as taxation. The fourth constitutional safeguard, the maxim of equal assessments, touched only taxation. Functionally a supplement to the maxim of shared burdens, equal assessments was the constitutional rule that Parliament imposed "all taxes in a general manner, so as not to tax any particular district or part of the kingdom, while the other parts of the kingdom are not taxed." Just as every section of the nation should be taxed equally, so should every type of property; nonelecting copyhold could not constitutionally be taxed differently from freehold held by electors. The rule meant there could be no taxes enacted in Great Britain and imposed on virtually represented nonelectors that were not equally imposed on members of Parliament and on their electors.[63]

There was no way the maxim of equal assessments could apply to parliamentary taxes placed on the American colonies for purpose of revenue. The Stamp Act, the Townshend duties, and the Tea Act lay tax burdens on the colonies alone. They relieved British taxpayers of the same burdens. If Americans became rich enough, the British could have been relieved of all burdens. To prevent that from occurring was the reason why the English-speaking people of the eighteenth century had constitutional law.

CHAPTER THREE

THE AUTHORITY TO LEGISLATE

Parliament attempted to end the debate over its authority to bind the colonies by legislation before the debate had really begun. When America's attention was focused on the issue of taxation and only beginning to concentrate on the authority to legislate, Parliament legislated that it had authority to bind the colonies in all cases whatsoever. By January 1766 the ministry knew the Stamp Act had to be repealed. There was resistance in Parliament, however, for many members agreed with Lord Chief Justice Mansfield that "the effect [of] repealing this Act" in response to American opposition would be "giving up the total Legislation of this Kingdom." To win over the opposition, repeal was preceded by the Declaratory Act, decreeing that Parliament "had, hath, and of right ought to have, full power and authority to make laws and statutes of sufficient force and validity to bind the colonies and people of *America* . . . in all cases whatsoever." "I consider this as the Way of Proceeding most consistent with your Dignity," the attorney general of England told the House of Commons. "I w[oul]d repeal not wantonly because it is asked, not timidly because it is resisted, but on being convinced of the Inexpediency, but I am clear on the Right. The sovereign Legislature must be supream."[1]

For adherents of the constitution of parliamentary command the Declaratory Act settled the constitutional dispute. For adherents of the constitution of customary rights the Declaratory Act was without legal substance. Americans did not react to the Declaratory statute as they had reacted to the stamp tax because, under the constitution of customary rights, there was no legal or constitutional grievance against which to react. American whigs, it should be remembered, did not challenge the Stamp Act as an abstract claim of right, but because it was about to be applied. Arguing that it was unconstitutional, they took to the streets to prevent enforcement, ensuring that the British would not have a precedent of taxation for purposes of revenue. There was no enforcement of the Declaratory Act to prevent. The statute was a declaration of constitutional principle, not the promulgation of a legislative program. Aside from the abstract claim, there was nothing in "litigation." Political theorists might think that if Americans did not treat the Declaratory Act as they did the Stamp Act, they risked conceding by acquiescence the right of Parliament's supremacy as claimed in the Declaratory Act. No eighteenth-century lawyer would have agreed.

Besides, American whigs believed the Declaratory Act was more words than substance. On each side of the Atlantic there was a widespread expectation that it would remain an abstract claim, that although the right might be defined and published in the statute books, it would not be exercised. "Let the matter of right rest upon the declaratory law, and say no more about it," a former governor of Massachusetts advised the House of Commons. The claim was even made by legislators in both Ireland and America that the colonists had been "told" or "assured" that the Declaratory Act would never be put to the test. If we are certain they were told no such thing, we still cannot rule out the possibility that they believed that were Lord Rockingham, then head of government, to say anything, he would give them this assurance.[2]

That American whigs felt no menace from the Declaratory Act does not mean it lacked constitutional purpose. Its passage was part and parcel of the repeal of the Stamp Act. As one side of two halves it appears, at first, ambiguous. The Declaratory Act told American whigs that Parliament claimed authority to legislate for them. The statute repealing the Stamp Act told the colonists that it was inexpedient to exercise that authority in certain circumstances. The two halves appear inconsistent from the perspective of the colonists. If we view them from the perspective of the crown, the Declaratory Act loses ambiguity. If the saving of the authority to legislate were to reserve supremacy over the monarchy as well as the colonies, the words "in all cases whatsoever" were, at least in respect to the king, as clear as any precisian could ask. The colonies were put on notice that their relationship with Great Britain was through Parliament and not through the crown alone as the colonists claimed—mutely in 1766 and loudly in 1775.[3]

In the nineteenth century Parliament would become omnipotent—to use an eighteenth-century term of derision[4]—for there were no constraints on its supremacy. By contrast, the constitution of customary rights as argued for in the eighteenth century had limits on supremacy. Again we must give close attention to the meaning and usage of words. Terms such as "supreme" and "supremacy" did not mean what some scholars assume them to mean. The concept of "supremacy" was more a topic of dispute than an element of legal definition. It was used as much to argue about constitutionalism as to explain it. "*Supremacy of Parliament* is a combination of terms unknown to the English polity," the earl of Abingdon contended. "The Legislature," he explained, "is a supreme, and may be called in one Sense an *absolute*, but in none an *arbitrary* Power." Abingdon was saying what many British common lawyers still said and what all American whigs said, that Parliament was bound by the "law" or the constitution or at least by unchangeable, customary, contractarian fundamental law.[5]

Legal uncertainty and constitutional anxiety often arose during the age of the American Revolution because one cherished constitutional principle collided with a second valued constitutional principle. One fundamental maxim, for example, was that the government of Great Britain was a limited, not an arbitrary, government. That rule, in turn, helps explain why the doctrine of supremacy to be "constitutional" had to have constraints. "It is a solecism in politics," Lord Abingdon pointed out, "to say that in a *limited* Government there can be *unlimited* Power." A competing principle was that sovereignty could have no gradations because in every government there had to be a supreme uncontrollable power vested in some person or institution. "There may be limited royalty," Samuel Johnson, a dictionary compiler, explained, "there may be limited counsulship; but there can be no limited government." It would not be for a generation or more after Johnson wrote that the obvious certainty of his constitutional doctrine would obtain universal acknowledgment—only on his side of the Atlantic. The fact that the jurisprudence of subordinating supremacy to constitutional law would soon be forgotten should not blind us to the fact it was still well understood in the age of the American Revolution. "When we say that the legislature is *supreme*," the mysterious British writer, *Junius*, explained, "we mean that it is the highest power known to the constitution;—that it is the highest in comparison with the other subordinate powers established by the laws." From that constitutional perspective the legal notion of supreme was still quite relative. "The power of the legislature," *Junius*, concluded, "is limited, not only by the general rules of natural justice, and the welfare of the community, but by the forms and principles of our particular constitution." There were at least six "forms" or "principles" of constraint limiting parliamentary supremacy: they were constraints of trust, constraints of consent, constraints of contract, constraints of constitutionalism, constraints of liberty, and constraints of law.[6]

The theory of constraint through delegated trust was discussed so often in the eighteenth century it could easily be made the subject of a separate study. For our purposes one example of the argument should be sufficient, and the following is especially pertinent as it is from the London press, reprinted in a Dublin magazine, discussing parliamentary legislation for North America. "The power of parliament," it was said, "is a power delegated by the people, to be always employed for their use and benefit, never to their disservice and injury." It was, therefore, a limited power, "bounded by the good and service of the people; and whenever such power shall be perverted to their hurt and detriment, the trust is broken, and becomes null and void."[7]

Closely related to constraints of trust were constraints of consent. The doctrine of consent to government made at least three important contributions to constitutional theory during the age of the American Revolution. The first was the notion that without consent to government there could be no liberty. The second was the legitimacy of government command. The right of government to command obedience to its laws was conferred by the people's consent to those laws. The third contribution was the most important. John Trenchard mentioned it in *Cato's Letters* when he said that the power of governments was limited by consent, and added that "[w]here positive Conditions were annexed to their Power, they were certainly bound by those Conditions." The very act of legitimization constrained authority. The fetters were outlined by two New England clergymen preaching in 1774. Government was created by people, Samuel Lockwood told Connecticut's assembly. "And when this is done by free consent, and mutual compact, it . . . limits the power of the rulers—secures the rights of the people—is the standard of justice for rulers, and subjects." In other words, Nathan Fiske pointed out in a sermon delivered in Brookfield, Massachusetts, there were fundamental laws marking the boundaries between the power of rulers, such as Parliament, and the liberties of the people. "And those can be no other than what are mutually agreed on, and consented to. Whatever authority therefore, the supreme power has to make laws . . . being an authority derived from the community and granted by them, can be justly exercised only within certain limits, and to a certain extent, according to agreement."[8]

We should not be misled by Fiske's use of the word "agreement." It makes eighteenth-century constitutional consent appear more direct or democratic than it was. When people then spoke of consent they meant constructive consent, such as the implied consent of an individual who, by living in British society, was said to consent to British rule and British law. Similar was the vicarious consent eighteenth-century Britons inherited from ancestors who, by conforming to the developing customs of an earlier day, consented to them. It was a consent, therefore, found in the doctrine of legal custom. Immemorial usage demonstrated the "consent" of generations. A peculiar expression of consent for American colonists was migration. A resident of Maryland consented to Maryland government when that person or that person's ancestor migrated to the colony.[9]

Whether actual or constructive, consent cut two ways. On one hand it explained why government was legitimate and people had to obey its commands. On the other hand it limited legitimacy to power that had been sanctioned by custom. Emigrants to Maryland had consented to be governed by the commands of Maryland's assembly, not by the commands of the Parliament in London.

Constraints of consent were reinforced by constraints of contract. When supposing government to be founded by consent of the people, as David Hume pointed out, the eighteenth century was supposing that there was an original contract. Again we can forget the social contract. It contributed little to the debate over Parliament's authority to bind the colonies in all cases whatsoever. Unlike the debate over taxation, however, only one original contract was important to the issue of legislation: the second original contract.

The imperial side of the debate made surprising use of the second original contract. "They went out subjects of Great Britain," Lord Lyttelton said of the first settlers of the colonies, "and unless they can shew a new compact made between them and the parliament of Great Britain (for the king alone could not make a new compact with them) they still are subjects to all intents and purposes whatsoever. If they are subjects, they are liable to the laws." As English citizens those settlers could have been represented in Parliament had they stayed in the British Isles. By settling in America, one writer explained, "they ceased to be represented here, and therefore *ought* to have a new Constitution similiar to that at home." But it was for them to have negotiated that new constitution and for their descendants to prove its terms. They had the burden of proof because their ancestors had not been foreigners. Being English they "well knew" that, if they did not contract new provisions, the old constitution of parliamentary rule would remain in force. "It is a pity," a pamphleteer lamented, "that things of this importance were not expressed in that clear manner so as not to be left doubtful."[10]

American whigs saw nothing doubtful. The second original contract negotiated by their ancestors was as clear as the second original contract the ancestors of the Anglo-Irish had negotiated before settling in Ireland. Ireland, like North America, had been colonized by English subjects who would never have left the mother country without contracting with the crown to keep all their English rights and privileges. Lord Lyttelton was anachronistic saying the king alone could not negotiate a second original contract. He had been speaking in 1766, long after the Glorious Revolution stripped the crown of many prerogatives. When the Irish and American settlers made their compacts the Tudor and Stuart monarchs could still bind the nation. The Irish settlers had made a contract; they had offered the king of England another kingdom for the guarantee of English constitutionalism. *"They granted* the Kingdom to *him;* and CHOSE and *acknowledged him,* as *their King;* and *he,* in return, *gave them,* the *same Laws* and *Privileges,* and, in general, the *same Constitution,* with *his English Subjects,* in all Points, by *which,* and *by none other,* they should be *for ever governed."* "By this Agreement," the lords of Ireland argued in 1719, "the People of *Ireland* obtained the Benefit of the *English* Laws, and many Privileges, particularly that of having a distinct Parliament here as in *England."*[11]

The colonial original contract was an exact duplication of the Irish original contract. The reason is not because the Americans knew of the Irish and copied it, but because both were extensions or novations of England's original contract. The authority of the second original contract had its greatest impact in the debate about legislation, partly because of the way that the negotiations were always described. They were between the crown and the original settlers, creating a constitutional relationship between king and people, not between the Americans and Parliament. "[T]he people of each Colony," the standard account explained, "either before or soon after their emigration, entered into particular compacts with the Kings of *England* to continue in allegiance to them, their heirs, and successors, and also as to their particular forms of Government, which appears by Charters, royal Proclamations, and the laws and regulations in each Colony, made by mutual consent of the King and the people." The proviso on legislation not only excluded Parliament but made the colonies autonomous, voters of Pembroke, Massachusetts, explained in 1773.

> *Resolved,* That although the British Parliament is the grand legislative of the nation, yet according to the original compact, solemnly made and entered into between the King of England and our ancestors, at the first coming into this country, and the present Royal Charter, no legislative authority can be exercised in or over this province, but that of the Great and General Court or Assembly, consisting of the King or his representative [*i.e.,* the governor], his Majesty's Council, and the House of Representatives.[12]

It would be well to consider just what was being claimed. Because for most citizens of the nation the exercise of consent was neither direct, personal, nor by elected representation, the true significance of the original contract is that it provided a stronger restraint on government in the eighteenth century than did representation, popular election, or the concept of consent. *"Humane Compact* must found *Government*: and yet be *superior* to it, so as to be its *Rule*," Bishop Benjamin Hoadly wrote in the first decade of the eighteenth century. The doctrine of the original contract and the second original contract, therefore, like the doctrine of trust and the doctrine of consent, was a theory or explanation of restraint on government power. It imposed restraint in several ways. One of the most utilized, as Lord Lyttelton indicated, was the imposition of the burden of proof. He had tried to impose it on those seeking to restrain government but the preferred practice put it on those asserting power. "As all lawful Government is founded in compact," a Philadelphian explained, "it behooves those who claim authority to prove they have it." On the matter of the authority of Parliament to legislate, American whigs easily assigned the burden. "Is there," the western Massachusetts lawyer Joseph Hawley asked, "any proof or evidence of any surrender, compact, or consent of the people, that the Colonies should be, *in all cases*, within the legislative authority of Parliament?" A second restraint was imposed by the very fact there was an original contract. Just to say that government had been created by contract was to claim there were restraints on power.[13]

It would not be too many years after the American Revolution that educated people in Great Britain would find arguments about the original contract and the second original contract fantastic. It may be assumed that they might have smiled if someone suggested that Parliament's sovereignty was limited by a "contract." Note, therefore, that in 1785, after the American Revolution had been fought and lost in the name of parliamentary supremacy, Great Britain's leading political theorist, William Paley, wrote that contractarian principles restrained the authority of the legislature. Because of contract, he contended, Britons thought of "laws, usages, or civil rights, as transcending the authority of the subsisting legislature, or possessing a force and sanction superior to what belong to the modern acts and edicts of the legislature." Paley, although interpreting the postrevolutionary British constitution, was still employing as British usage what soon would be only the American meaning of words.[14]

The same point can be made about the constraints of constitutionalism. Although we think of them as belonging to the British constitutional past they were spoken of in the age of the American Revolution as if the constitution of customary rights was the country's only constitution. Consider what Edmund Burke was thinking when, the year after Yorktown, he wrote: "Our constitution is a prescriptive constitution; it is a constitution whose sole authority is that it has existed time out of mind. . . . Your king, your lords, your judges, your juries, grand and little, all are prescriptive. . . . Prescription is the most solid of all titles, not only to property, but, which is to secure that property, to government." By the next half century, no one, not even American common lawyers would speak of a citizen's "title" to government or of prescription being the "sole authority" for governmental command.[15]

We may know that Burke's constitutionalism was archaic, but that is hindsight. It seems doubtful if many of Burke's contemporaries realized it. The concept of constitutionalism as a restraint on power was still viable in Great Britain during the years of the American Revolution, pervading the way Britons conceived of government, of government's authority, and of governmental legitimacy. They spoke not only of the British constitution or the imperial constitution, but of the constitution of institutions, such as the constitution of Parliament, which, in the language of constitutionalism, was a way of discussing limitations imposed by innate structure rather than by extrinsic restraint. "The limit therefore to the supreme legislative power is that which limits every other nature, the principle of its constitution," William Jones wrote in 1768. "That it shall preserve its form;—that it shall maintain inviolate the freedom of election:—that it shall employ the public force for the preservation of equal liberty; are the laws to which it is subject, because they are the laws of its nature. These laws it cannot transgress, without changing its character, without ceasing to be that which it is, a government by consent." It is worth recalling that Jones's thoughts were shaped by the law of the eighteenth century. He did not deny that Parliament was sovereign, or that its command was all powerful. His limits were inherent limits of purpose, of function, and of constitutionalism.[16]

Commentators on the constitution like Jones were common in the second half of the eighteenth century, yet we may wonder if we understand them. They knew that the all-powerful Parliament was without external restraints yet insisted that it was constrained by constitutionalism. Perhaps they could not face constitutional reality. If Parliament had become sovereign over the law and the constitution then the worst fear of British constitutionalists, something that had been dreaded since the days of Charles I and Oliver Cromwell, had come to pass. British government had become arbitrary. That fear is the answer to a question that as yet has not been asked: why did the dichotomy of the two British constitutions exist? The best explanation is that most Britons could not bring themselves to admit that the constitution of customary rights had been overcome by the constitution of sovereign command and the reason they could not admit it was because to do so meant they were living under an arbitrary government.

We have seen how arbitrary power related to eighteenth-century constitutionalism. The topic was discussed at the end of the first chapter. One point made was that avoiding arbitrariness was but another way of describing constitutionalism. Britons and Americans still agreed about that but they were drawing apart on the question of how to define "unconstitutional" arbitrariness. The British were slowly coming to accept the conclusion that legislative power could be constitutional even though arbitrary. Put in precise legal theory, as the eighteenth century drew to a close, the British were beginning to have constitutional problems with the notion that a supreme, sovereign Parliament with authority in all cases whatsoever could be arbitrary. Consider the thoughts of Sir William Meredith when telling the House of Commons in 1777 that the reason the American colonies had rebelled was Parliament's insistence that it was legislatively supreme. "No man can deny in theory the supreme, unlimited power of the British legislature; but the execution of that power is a trust delegated by the people, and to be guided by the principles of liberty and justice." Here is an example of constitutional thought no longer voiced today but once prevalent in eighteenth-century jurisprudence: the apparent contradiction of unlimited power limited by the concept of liberty. Liberty was one of the elements along with trust, consent, contract, and constitutionalism that was a constraint limiting legislative authority. "The Governour, Council, and House of Representatives, which comprise the Assembly," Joseph Hawley wrote of colonial legislatures, explaining why they could not alter "the fundamentals" of government, "are creatures of, and derive all their power from a Constitution agreed upon and previously established, which has for its *primum mobile*, groundwork and leading principle, Liberty, civil and religious. All transactions therefore, growing out of such a Constitution, must breathe the spirit of freedom, and be governed by it, as by a pole-star in the political hemisphere."[17]

Hawley thought he was speaking of the constraint of liberty on parliamentary authority, but today we recognize he was concerned with the rule of law, the procedural apparatus by which liberty was defended. The argument was more important than Hawley realized. It was on the very issue of Parliament's claim to supremacy over law that American concerns for the rule of law had come to differ from British concerns. In British constitutional theory, concerns about the rule of law almost entirely focused on the executive. The concept of the rule of law was a barrier constraining the power of the crown and not the power of Parliament. In fact, more and more in Great Britain the concept of rule of law was being equated with Parliament's command. The British refusal to join colonial whigs in extending the concept of the rule of law from constraining the crown to constraining Parliament summed up much of the American Revolution's constitutional controversy. The difference was delineated in a Philadelphia pamphlet published in the same year as the Declaration of Independence. "No country can be called *free* which is governed by an absolute power," the pamphleteer contended; "and it matters not whether it be an absolute royal power or an absolute legislative power, as the consequences will be the same to the people."[18]

The Philadelphian was talking good American constitutional theory. In the seventeenth-century it had also been good English constitutional theory. Not only was it losing favor in Great Britain during the closing decades of the eighteenth century, but it may not be an exaggeration to say it was no longer understood. In respect to Parliament, the concept of liberty had taken on a new meaning in the mother country that was alien to colonial whig thought. "I knew [sic] what liberty is," a British merchant told an American. "Is it not the representation of the whole *British* empire by *King, Lords*, and Commons?" Of course it was, especially if one remembered that Parliament had been metamorphosed into the embodiment of liberty at the Glorious Revolution. It was to those two seventeenth-century triumphs of constitutionalism—the Revolution of 1688 and its political settlement—that eighteenth-century Britons traced contemporary constitutional liberty. The balances of the mixture worked into the tripartite Parliament had ended the British constitutionalist's ancient fear of arbitrariness. The members of the two houses—or of the House of Commons alone—had become the "Guardians of Liberty and the Laws" for all British people. It did not matter who elected the members. What mattered was that they were elected according to constitutional custom and were constitutionally representative. "The spirit of our English constitutional liberty," a London pamphlet explained in 1771, "is founded upon annual exercise of our elective rights; and not in having, a fixed representative body of men, in parliament." The coming nineteenth-century British idea would be that liberty required an extensive suffrage or, contrary to what eighteenth-century Americans still claimed, that it did not require the power to legislate be limited. Indeed, the emerging British theory was the opposite. Liberty was maintained by the very exercise of parliamentary legislation. "British liberties are in general secured by the *acts of the British parliament*." Put another way, from the British perspective rule of law now meant rule by Parliament. From the American perspective rule by Parliament would make rule of law constitutionally meaningless.[19]

Because the emerging British reformulation of rule of law was never prominently articulated, Americans may not have appreciated how deep the gulf had become. The realization that some British now defined liberty as parliamentary legislation could have staggered American constitutionalists had the fact sunk into their legal consciousness. They and their descendants—even to the end of the twentieth century—would never break free of the fundamentals of anti-Stuart constitutionalism in which power unrestrained was not legal. They could not see what difference it made for power to be legislative rather than monarchical. "There cannot be a more dangerous doctrine adopted in a state, than to admit that the legislative authority has a right to alter the constitution," another Philadelphian wrote in 1776. "For as the constitution limits the authority of the legislature; if the legislature can alter the constitution, they can give themselves what bounds they please." He was describing the coming British constitution.[20]

History taught Britons that they had to put their confidence in an institution that Americans, starting with the Stamp Act, felt they could not trust. Both sides thought they had the same goals—avoidance of unrestrained arbitrary power—and both used the same word, *limits*. "The parliament has a right to make all law within the limits of their own constitution," the colonists repeated over and over again. The British agreed that the problem was a matter of "limits," but they no longer believed there were constitutional reasons to set parliamentary limits. The limits on Parliament's jurisdiction were inherent in the very nature or "law" of the institution itself. It was an ambivalent notion, owing something to traditional common-law ways of thinking, such as the implied restraints of the original contract, and much to a reluctance by constitutionalists in the eighteenth century to think through the ramifications of parliamentary power.[21]

The various constraints of liberty, consent, trust, and constitutionalism that the constitution of customary rights imposed on the authority of parliament were principles and maxims of law that colonial whigs said were still valid. To make their case they sometimes turned to past events for evidence of current law and when doing so gave the appearance of discussing history. Generally they were using history but using it as law, not history. The distinction is best delineated by considering the debate over precedents of parliamentary legislation and the meaning of those precedents. Both sides, American whigs and British parliamentary imperialists, cited precedents of past parliamentary legislation binding on the colonies either to prove that parliaments before the 1760s had not enacted statutes intended to govern the colonies internally or to prove that earlier parliaments had not only promulgated such statutes but had exercised legitimate constitutional authority when doing so.

Discussion of precedents of legislation fell into two categories, general precedents and precedents of specific legislation. The general precedents were also of two sorts, "precedents of charter" and "precedents of analogy." The first involved arguments about the intention of English kings when the colonies were first incorporated, whether they were to be constitutionally associated only with the crown, or whether the understanding had been that despite being authorized to constitute legislative assemblies they were also to be governed by parliamentary command.[22] Second were "precedents of analogy," provided by the Channel Islands and Ireland. These precedents established authority for colonial legislative autonomy from the era before the crown shared the governance of the "realm" with Parliament. It was on the issue of Parliament's authority to bind the colonies in all cases whatsoever that the analogy of Ireland was extensively discussed. On the whole, the Irish analogy as it related to parliamentary power was less a constitutional than a political consideration. Irish history and government warned Americans why they should avoid parliamentary rule but did not furnish definitive authority either way for legislative autonomy.[23]

Little would be added to our knowledge by considering each of the precedents of direct legislation that were debated. We can learn more about the eighteenth-century constitution and the revolutionary controversy by considering the technique of arguing precedents of history and then summarizing some typical examples. The role played by history in the constitutional controversy is often misunderstood, reason enough to give the subject attention.

Jonathan Sewall, attorney general of Massachusetts, imperial judge of admiralty, and one of the best colonial lawyers to remain loyal to the British crown after the Declaration of Independence, believed that the constitutionality of parliamentary sovereignty over North America could be proven or disproved by historical evidence. "And from this view we shall also perceive whether the present claim of parliament is new, as many ignorantly suppose, or whether it was made, openly and expressly, before the grant of the [second Massachusetts] charter, and has ever since been uniformly exercised by them, and acknowledged by us." That was the type of "historical" evidence developed and argued by both sides, evidence not just of specific legislation and recorded actions, but of attitudes both of individuals and generations about parliamentary supremacy. At first the methodology looks like history employed to argue constitutional law, but on closer examination it proves to be not history according to the historical method but that most maligned version of history, forensic history.[24]

The technique was to cite an event, a statement, or a document, to discuss how the cited material related to an issue of constitutional law, and then to argue this material not as evidence of constitutional history but as legal authority, much like a common-law precedent. Negative evidence that something had not occurred was as authoritative as was evidence of actual historical happenings. General, sweeping suppositions were as seriously argued as were documented instances of opposition to parliamentary authority.[25] And both sides of the constitutional debate took these arguments seriously. The imperial side cited precedents of legislation as extensively as American whigs denied their relevance, as well the imperialists might for the precedents supporting Parliament's authority to bind the colonies in all cases whatsoever were much more persuasive than were the precedents supporting the authority of taxation. In truth, had the issue turned on the premises of the constitution of customary rights alone, and had there been no claim that Parliament possessed sovereign power, precedents of legislation would have been the strongest part of London's case.

The case would have been far from certain. The best part of the imperialist precedents were those that were precedents of regulation. There was no disputing these precedents. Ever since the Commonwealth period of Oliver Cromwell's rule, Parliament had enacted legislation not only regulating American trade with customs duties, but directing with whom Americans could conduct commerce, where American ships could sail, and what products Americans could import and export. Often this legislation was intended to benefit some other parts of the empire (the sugar islands or the home islands, for example) at the expense of the North American colonies. The constitutional issue was not whether these laws were valid precedents of Parliament's authority to bind the colonies in these situations but whether they were authority to bind the colonies in all cases whatsoever. Colonial whigs, drawing an analogy to their argument that import taxes for the purpose of regulating trade were constitutional, contended that statutes regulating trade were not precedents of Parliament's authority to bind in all cases whatsoever. In the words of the Continental Congress, Americans "did not complain" even though these laws were often "grievous."[26]

To understand the American Revolution we should pay closer attention to what colonial assemblies said about Parliament's authority to regulate trade. Their phraseology was carefully crafted, and if studied with equal care shows that although whig legislators raised objections to Parliament's regulation of trade they never raised constitutional objections. Distinctions should be made between arguments that Parliament did not possess power to promulgate a statute and that it promulgated a economically harsh, unfair, or unworkable—yet constitutional—statute. A typical instance was the instructions of South Carolina's Convention for its delegates to the Continental Congress, telling them to work for repeal of all acts that "lay unnecessary restraints and burthens on trade." The members of the Convention knew that when they voted to have Congress ask Parliament to reform a trade law they were acknowledging Parliament's authority to legislate. When the colonists objected to *constitutional* legislation that they thought costly, unfair, or unreasonable, they complained about Parliament's policy, not Parliament's jurisdiction. Even grievances such as commercial monopoly or unequal treatment between favored and less favored parts of the empire that might have been turned into constitutional issues were complained of on trade grounds if possible. The objection voiced was to the monopoly or the unequal treatment, not to Parliament's power to regulate trade.[27]

There is no need to pursue further the precedents of regulation. Their precedential value depended on the validity of the trade-regulation distinction. For those believing the distinction without constitutional merit, statutes of regulation such as the various Navigation acts and other trade laws provided the British with good, proven, convincing precedents for Parliament's authority to bind the colonies in all cases whatsoever. For American whigs the same precedents proved only Parliament's authority to legislate for the colonies in matters of trade regulation. If they were precedents for anything in controversy, colonial whigs said, they were precedents proving colonial legislative autonomy, not parliamentary sovereign command. The difference lay not in a disagreement about the meaning or operation of the statutes, but in the theory of why they were constitutional. What set the laws of trade regulation apart from the other statutes enacted by Parliament was that all colonists, whigs as well as loyalists, conceded that the laws were constitutional.

Precedents of legislation that were not concerned with trade regulation were quite a different precedential category. Again, we are faced with the constitutional puzzle why imperialists, especially writers and speakers retained to promote the imperial government's side, depended on statutory precedents to prove what one cabinet minister called Great Britain's "right to regulate the internal concerns of America." At best, enacted and enforced statutes were authority under the old constitution of prescriptive, customary rights. They were much less significant, perhaps even irrelevant, as authority under the constitution of sovereign command. So how do we account for the fact that imperialists, including ministerial hacks who obtained income writing political tracts on behalf of the administration, made as much of these precedents as their opponents did? One answer might be that imperialists thought their case so strong that they might as well argue the law of the old constitution and persuade the colonial whigs that the American argument was wrong. If so, it would suggest they believed that the American whigs were sincere about the constitution and that they were not using law as a smoke screen for other motivations such as economic independence or nationalism. Another answer is that they, like so many other people in Great Britain, thought the customary constitution still law.

Precedents of nonregulatory legislation fell under two general categories. One was precedents of quasi-legislation, the other precedents of internal legislation. The statutes of quasi-legislation were by far the more numerous and included "An Act to Punish Governors of Plantations . . . for Crimes," the Mutiny Act governing the British military in the colonies, several laws prohibiting cutting trees reserved for the Royal Navy, the Post Office Act which imposed criminal penalties for abuse of the mails and required ferrymen to transport letter carriers across streams, and legislation regulating the collection of debts which not only preempted colonial laws but determined the jurisdiction of law suits tried in colonial courts and limited the process that could be applied. These and similar laws operated in North America, altering the private property rights and personal entitlements of citizens. Imperialists cited them as precedents for Parliament's authority to bind the colonies in all cases whatsoever. American whigs distinguished them on the grounds that they were laws of general superintendence, not of particular internal legislation, and hence properly within the purview of London's authority to regulate. It is not profitable to discuss them all. Instead, consider the most persuasive precedent in this category—parliamentary restrictions upon colonial bills of credit and other forms of paper money. They are the strongest precedents of quasi-legislation because they were instances of Parliament legislation for the internal governance of the colonies. We can concentrate on just one of these statutes as typical of the constitutional issues and the legislative maneuvering that characterized all of the precedents of quasi-legislation.

The most significant instance of Parliament's attempts to control colonial credit and legal tender by direct legislation is the "Act to regulate and restrain Paper Bills of Credit" in New England. The act's legislative history is revealing, showing how important some people regarded the issues of constitutionality even before those issues became subject to trans-Atlantic controversy. The financial "evil" that the act sought to correct was that New England "bills of credit have, for many years past, been depreciating in their value, by means whereof all debts of late years have been paid and satisfied with a much less value than was contracted for," all of which could cause instability in imperial trade. If one considered only that purpose, the precedential category of the act would be trade regulation or imperial superintendence, and American whigs could have claimed the act was not a precedent of direct, internal legislation. If, however, one considered the mechanics of executing the act, the precedential category could be internal legislation. The act was a direct injunction on the New England assemblies, prohibiting them from creating "any paper bills or bills of credit" and prohibiting "relief" legislation by requiring that private debts, including those owed to fellow Americans, be paid "according to the terms of such loans respectively, and the true intent and meaning thereof."[28]

The act had a second bit of revealing legislative history. When first proposed in the 1730s its reception was so mixed that it would later be claimed as a precedent by constitutionalists on both sides of the American Revolution dispute. Arguing that it was a precedent for Parliament's authority to legislate internally for North America, John Lind, a pamphleteer serving North's administration during the revolutionary controversy, contended that Richard Partridge, who had been the official agent to Parliament for two colonies at the time the legislation was being enacted into law, had not raised constitutional objections. "Did he call in question the right of parliament to make this regulation?" Lind asked. "Was it on any pretended exemption from parliamentary authority that he grounded his objections to the bill? No such thing. All he ventured to do was to apply himself to the equity of parliament, by insinuating that the provisions of the bill were contrary to the privileges of the colony."[29]

Lind was "shading" the evidence. It was true that, when petitioning as agent for Pennsylvania, a colony not covered by the legislation, Partridge had raised economic, not constitutional objections. But when petitioning on behalf of Rhode Island, one of the New England colonies directly affected by the proposed legislation, he had argued legal objections. The bill, he charged, "would effect the said [Rhode Island] charter, and some of the most valuable privileges thereby granted to the inhabitants of the said colony." He was referring to the Rhode Island Assembly's legislative autonomy which would have been seriously abrogated once the bill was enacted.[30]

It is surprising that Lind suppressed this evidence. From the imperial perspective, it could have strengthened his side of the controversy to show that in the 1730s, colonial agents had protested the constitutionality of the bill against bills of credit, yet despite these objections Parliament went ahead and enacted it. Of course, from the opposite perspective, the argument could have been made that this evidence showed that, long before 1765, American agents had been on guard against the constitutional threat posed by parliamentary legislation. The last argument was by no means as strong in law as the direct precedent that the imperialists could cite, but for what it was worth, it strengthened the American whig case, at least to the extent of showing that case had been argued under different constitutional circumstances, and not concocted to meet the challenge of the new brand of imperial legislation Parliament had begun to promulgate with the Stamp Act.

In April 1764, the "Act to regulate and restrain Paper Bills of Credit" received additional strength as a precedent supporting Parliament's authority to legislate in all cases whatsoever. It was expanded from restricting the legislative autonomy of only four New England colonies, to restricting lawmaking in all the mainland colonies. The extension was promulgated by the so-called Currency Act, permitting bills then in circulation to continue as legal tender but mandating retirement on the expiration date previously set by local statute and prohibiting issuance of new paper in any form.

The colonists raised the predictable constitutional (as well as economic) objections to the Currency Act. They are obvious and need not be detailed. There was, however, an issue raised that deserves notice. The Currency Act was one of seven parliamentary statutes that the Continental Congress voted "subversive of American rights." That constitutional objection defined the official position of all the colonies except for the New York General Assembly when, in March 1775, it restated colonial grievances. "We . . . think," the New York legislators petitioned George III, "the act prohibiting the legislature of this colony from passing any law for the emission of *paper currency*, to be legal tender therein, is disadvantageous to the growth and commerce thereof; an abridgment of your Majesty's prerogative (in the preservation of which we are deeply interested) and a violation of our legislative rights."[31]

It is risky to evaluate how much a petition of one colonial assembly reflected American whig constitutional thought in general, but in this case it is a risk worth taking. It is unlikely that the New York legislators expressed ideas peculiar to themselves for their constitutional argument, especially their remarkable statement that they were "deeply interested" in the preservation of the king's "prerogative," was well within mainstream American whig constitutional thought. They were saying that the regulation of paper money was a matter properly within the purview of imperial superintendence, but as part of the Crown's authority to govern rather than Parliament's authority to legislate. It was the prerogative, constitutionally exercised through the governor's veto and the Privy Council's power of disallowing colonial legislation, that alone had constitutional authority to enforce imperial policy governing legal tender. If we take into account the general constitutional theory of American whigs and the role they assigned the Crown in the governance of the empire, the conclusion could be that the New York General Assembly more accurately expressed the American whig constitutional grievance against the Currency Act than did the Continental Congress which settled for the ambiguous complaint that the statute was "subversive of American rights."

The final category of precedents of internal legislation enacted before 1763 concerned precedents directly on point: Parliament making law for the internal governance of the colonies, the strongest precedents for establishing Parliament's constitutional right to legislate in all cases whatsoever. There were three. One was the Hat Act of 1732 forbidding the export of beaver hats from any colony, even to a second colony or to any other destination within the empire. The second was the Iron Act. It was similar in intent to the Hat Act, giving a monopoly to British manufacturers. The third, the Woolen Act, did the same. All three were blatant instances of home favoritism. All three were economically oppressive to the potential promise of American industry. And all three were obeyed without constitutional protest in the colonies.

The significance as precedents of legislation of these three acts for the adherents of parliamentary sovereignty can be summed up by a claim made for the Hat Act in 1775. "This act," the author of *The Supremacy of the British Legislature over the Colonies* contended, "is the more striking, as it shows that parliament exerted their authority in the internal regulations of the provinces in America; and the ready submission of the Americans to this act, notwithstanding its severity, is an acknowledgment of the right of parliament so to do." Colonial whigs disagreed. None of these acts was among the constitutional grievances that the first Continental Congress demanded be

66   THE AUTHORITY TO LEGISLATE

repealed. Nor were they mentioned in the Declaration of Independence. Compiling a list of the six major *economic* statutes that he termed "wantonly oppressive," Virginia's Arthur Lee included all three. Even though economically oppressive they were not unconstitutional. In fact Lee turned the argument around and cited them as proof that Americans would obey Parliament's constitutional legislation no matter how damaging to colonial economic well being.[32]

For American whigs like Arthur Lee, even these three acts of unquestioned *internal* legislation were precedents of constitutional regulation, not precedents for Parliament's authority to bind the colonies in all cases whatsoever. For defenders of parliamentary supremacy, by contrast, all statutes mentioning the colonies that Parliament had promulgated since at least the Restoration of Charles II to the English throne were evidence of Parliament's constitutional jurisdiction. "The truth is," *Benevolus* told the *London Chronicle*, "that all acts of the British legislature, expres[s]ly extended to the colonies, have ever been received there as laws, and executed in their courts, the right of parliament to make them, being never yet contested, acts to raise money upon the colonies by internal taxes only and alone excepted."[33] *Benevolus*'s argument, a conclusive statement of law, could have settled the controversy, at least for imperialists, had they found it persuasive. In fact, about the only people who seem to have thought that this law resolved the question have been twentieth-century scholars. Rather than rest on the authority of precedents, Parliament did the opposite. Because its authority was challenged and had to be shored up, Parliament took the legislative offensive. It enacted and sought to enforce legislation of supremacy: statutes designed to support its authority to bind the colonies in all cases whatsoever.

The primary instance of legislation of supremacy, the Declaratory Act, can be ignored. American whigs, after all, ignored it, making certain it was never part of the revolutionary debate. They did not, however, ignore the other four pieces of legislation Parliament passed to promulgate its supremacy: three statutes and a set of resolutions. They were the Act of 7 George III suspending the legislative authority of the New York General Assembly, resolutions to enforce the Act of 35 Henry VIII authorizing trials within the realm for treason committed outside the realm, the Townshend Acts which included the tea tax, and the Tea Act. They were not haphazardly enacted, but were part of a deliberate, calculated imperial legal strategy. They were also a bit of constitutional derring-do. In fact, from one perspective, the law suspending the New York General Assembly and the Tea Act were potentially the most constitutionally risky statutes enacted by Parliament during the revolutionary controversy. The New York law, the great legal writer Sir William Blackstone noted with satisfaction, was designed to carry "into effect" the "authority" of the Declaratory Act, and the Tea Act, when considered as legislating Parliament's supremacy, was nothing more or less than the Declaratory Act executed.

Had American whigs no strategy of constitutional avoidance, Parliament would not have had to enact the statute suspending the authority of the New York General Assembly. It was because colonial whigs, seeking to avoid precedents of parliamentary supremacy, tried to keep the Mutiny Act from becoming a precedent of internal legislation, that Parliament, in part to obtain a precedent, suspended the New York General Assembly. The Mutiny Act governing the British military in North America required that the colonies furnish soldiers stationed within their borders with certain enumerated necessities. Here was an instance of direct internal legislation to the most extreme degree. Requiring that local assemblies vote funds for specific purposes was a remarkable combination of direct legislation and indirect parliamentary taxation.[34]

The Mutiny Act did not pose an economic issue. The sums involved were so small they were not worth political contention. It was the constitutional principle that teemed with peril, although not all whigs were equally alarmed. Even after passage of the Stamp Act some assemblies voted the funds requisitioned by their governors, either because they had requested that the troops be sent to their jurisdiction or because they were not troubled by the constitutional implications. Others, wanting to avoid a constitutional confrontation with London, yet determined to avoid what Georgia's Commons House of Assembly called "founding a precedent," provided funds in a manner that, although satisfying the requisition, did not comply with the specific terms of the Mutiny Act. In some cases they voted stipends for troops instead of furnishing the itemized supplies requested, even specifying precise amounts to be paid officers and men as individuals, or they provided only part of the money required, or only some of the supplies, deliberately omitting items enumerated in the Mutiny Act, or they did not mention the Mutiny Act or the provisions in the Act, creating a record of supplying the troops but not of complying with Parliament's command. The strategy turned on small technical points, allowing American whigs—as Parliament and several governors complained—to claim that the assemblies had not, as a matter of precedent, obeyed the Mutiny Act.[35]

London's tolerance of this strategy ended when New York legislators voted funds for some of the enumerated supplies but not for others. The General Assembly gave the excuse that these items were not provided in some other parts of the empire, but it was well understood in London that the Assembly wanted the grant to "appear a voluntary act of their own, and not done in obedience to an act of parliament." In other words, they intended to avoid giving Parliament a precedent of obedience.[36] The year was

1767. The colonists had already forced repeal of the Stamp Act and were about to force the repeal of the Townshend duties, and Parliament decided it had to take a stand by asserting its legislative supremacy. It passed a statute "suspending" New York's legislative authority "until provision shall have been made . . . for furnishing his Majesty's Troops within the said province with all such necessaries as are required by the said acts of parliament." The sole purpose was obedience. Some observers supposed that, once New York obeyed, "the Mutiny Act will probably be suffered to expire silently by its own limitation, and be no more revived." That law was simply not worth the trouble if enforcement meant yearly battles with colonial assemblies uneasy with its implications of parliamentary supremacy. What Parliament in effect did was instruct the governor of New York to approve no bills passed by the General Assembly until it complied with the Mutiny Act. It was a drastic departure from constitutional practice for Parliament to instruct a governor. That was the king's prerogative and had never been a legislative function. It was also unnecessary, Pennsylvania's John Dickinson protested. "The crown might have restrained the governor of *New-York*, even from calling the assembly together, by its prerogative in the royal governments." Parliament, he complained, was asserting "the *supreme authority* of the *British* legislature over the colonies." That was precisely what Parliament intended—authority over all the colonies.[37]

Before the Suspending Act went into operation, the New York General assembly informed Governor Henry Moore—or so Moore reported to London—that it would comply with "the Act of Parliament." Moore soon learned his mistake. The bill the legislators voted met only one of the objections that had been raised to the previous requisition. It "made an appropriation of such a sum as was thought necessary to furnish the articles" enumerated in the Mutiny Act. "[N]o particular mention was made" of these articles, the governor lamented, "nor of the money being raised in consequence of the Act of Parliament, there being only a bare recital of the Sum ordered to be paid into the hands of General Gage for the use of His Majesty's Troops quartered here." Moore was so chagrined that he "resolved" to veto the bill. Circumstances forced him "to change my resolution," for some of the troops were preparing to leave the colony and their officers, who had been paying for supplies out of their own pockets, might never be reimbursed if he did not accept this money. The military apparently put great pressure on Moore, for, disobeying his instructions, he signed the legislation and passed the controversy back to London.[38]

The British administration faced a difficult political decision. Everyone knew that the New York grant was not an acknowledgment of parliamentary supremacy, but as the Suspending Act had not called specifically for acknowledgment, New York's noncompliance could be winked at and called compliance. The question was submitted to the law officers who took the road of narrow construction. As "the only Object" of the Suspending Act was "fully accomplished by the Supply of Money," they ruled that the terms of the act had been satisfied. It is important to understand that to say that the New York General Assembly avoided acknowledging supremacy, yet satisfied the Suspending Act by giving the ministry something to "wink" at, is not the same as saying that the General Assembly did not vigorously oppose the claim by Parliament to legislate internally for the colonies as embodied by the Mutiny Act. The Assembly, in fact, opposed the Suspending Act on the only two grounds that were constitutionally significant: by ignoring Parliament's assertion of supremacy and by not acknowledging Parliament's supremacy. Parliament had legislated its supremacy over the colonies and, when the ministry overlooked the fact that New York was technically in noncompliance, it failed to obtain the precedent it sought. True there had been a compliance. The prescribed amount of money had been voted by the New York General Assembly. But the wording of the grant was at most a technical compliance with the New York Suspending Act, not the good-faith compliance with the Mutiny Act that Parliament needed. As a former prime minister complained, no one could call "the Conduct to the Assembly of New York in giving a sum of money to the Crown but refusing to take the least Notice of the mutiny act . . . a Submission to that law."[39]

Parliament's second legislation of supremacy was technically a joint resolution of the two houses. Troubled by disturbances in Massachusetts Bay over the Townshend duties and the seizure for customs violations by the British navy of John Hancock's sloop *Liberty* while docked in Boston harbor,[40] the Commons and the Lords resolved that the king obtain evidence so the government could prosecute *in England*, offenses committed in Massachusetts "pursuant to the provisions of the statute of the 35th year of the reign of King Henry VIII, in case your majesty shall, upon receiving such information, see sufficient ground for such proceeding."

The Act of 35 Henry VIII, promulgated over two hundred years before, provided that "all . . . treasons, misprisons of treasons, or concealments of treasons" committed "out of this realm of *England*" were cognizable in England as if committed "within the same shire where they shall be so enquired of, heard, and determined." The resolutions were a drastic assertion of legislative supremacy. Although not enacting a new statute, Parliament was saying that committing treason, not reporting a known act of treason, or concealment of treason were all crimes which, when committed in North America and competently cognizable by a court of the colony where committed, could, by the authority of Parliament first pronounced in 1543, result in the removal for trial to the former Kingdom of England, divesting colonial courts and juries of jurisdiction. Parliament was asserting the strongest claim to supremacy it would make between passage of the Declaratory Act and passage of the coercive acts.[41]

By resurrecting the Act of 35 Henry VIII Parliament was showing respect for the constitution of customary rights. Had the ministry been thinking only of the constitution of sovereign command it would have enacted new legislation easing the task of enforcement by vesting authority in imperial officials who had not existed in 1543. Instead, to gain the aura of established precedent, it invoked an ancient statute limited to the definitions of law prevalent at the time of enactment. Although seemingly respectful of American constitutional theory, Parliament's strategy was not successful. The law of 35 Henry VIII, intended to legislate Parliament's supremacy over the colonies, had the opposite effect. If we consider the numerous colonial assembly and town-meeting resolutions passed in reaction, it would not be an exaggeration to say that the statute of Henry, more than any other issue, except for taxation and the coercive acts, forced Americans to think about the implications of legislative sovereignty. Some of the most extreme claims of the right of the colonies to be legislatively autonomous of Parliament were drafted to protest the Act of 35 Henry VIII. Compelled by London to confront the issue of supremacy, some American legislators claimed exclusive criminal jurisdiction, something they otherwise would have left unsaid. The Act of 35 Henry VIII, South Carolina's Commons House of Assembly bluntly stated, could not extend to the colonies "where there is sufficient provision by the laws of the land, for the impartial trial of all such persons as are charged with" treason, misprison of treason, or concealment of treason. 35 Henry VIII was universally condemned in the colonies, with most assemblies agreeing, at least by implication, with the elected representatives of Delaware and North Carolina, who called the act both "unconstitutional and illegal."[42]

The Townshend duties were legislation designed to assert Parliament's authority to command. Because the income from the duties was earmarked to pay local colonial officials previously paid by the colonial assemblies, the Townshend Acts, had they been successful, would have altered the internal governance of the colonies. "[B]y raising a revenue for the support of the civil government, you destroy the utility of the Assemblies," a former governor of Massachusetts told the House of Commons. "[I]t operates as a revocation of the rights and privileges of the legislatures of those colonies, as they have been permitted hitherto to enjoy them."[43]

When the Townshend Acts failed to produce revenue their repeal was used by Parliament to legislate supremacy once again. Because of American opposition to the law, the ministry could not consider total repeal. There had to be colonial submission, the House of Commons was told. Connecticut's agent summed up the debate: "they [the cabinet] thought it absolutely necessary to assert and maintain their supremacy over them [the colonists]; that that supremacy was denied, and their [Parliament's] authority disputed . . . that to submit to them [*i.e.*, to repeal the duties without qualification] was to give up Parliament and all its authority into the hands of the Americans."[44]

The constitutional doctrine guiding the ministry could be called "bastard precedent" or "surreptitious precedent." It was the legal principle holding that repeal of legislation to quiet constitutional opposition to that legislation, was, in constitutional effect, an adoption of the arguments of that opposition; that is, to have repealed the Stamp Act without qualifying repeal with the Declaratory Act would have provided American whigs with a surreptitious precedent of Parliament admitting that it was unconstitutional to tax the colonies internally for purposes of revenue. By the same principle, outright repeal of the Townshend duties, without some qualification, such as claiming the tax was "anti-commercial" or retaining one duty as a token of supremacy, could have become a precedent supporting the constitutional pretensions of American whigs to internal legislative autonomy. That was why Lord Hillsborough, the secretary of state for the colonies, became annoyed when Connecticut demanded repeal on constitutional grounds. "Had they petitioned on the ground of inexpediency only," he said of Connecticut's Assembly, "they would have succeeded, but while you call in question the right, we cannot hear you." Meeting with agents of all the colonies, Hillsborough assured them that the way to obtain repeal was to drop "the point of right," "that if they [the colonies] would *waive* the point of right, and petition for a repeal of the duties as *burdensome and grievous*, Administration was disposed to come into it." The colonies refused and for the same reason motivating the ministry: fear of creating a surreptitious precedent. "[I]t was objected," Connecticut's agent explained, "that silence upon so essential a point might perhaps be construed a consent to waive, at least, if not give up the right." The constitutional controversy over supremacy was in danger of becoming mired in the concept of right. There were only two solutions: one side could surrender the right, or one side could back away from conflict, avoiding a surreptitious precedent by saving its claim to right.[45]

Exercising constitutional caution, the ministry broke the impasse. Just as American whigs had refused to give Parliament the precedent that it had wanted of obedience to the Townshend legislation, Parliament refused to give the whigs the precedent they wanted, unconditional and outright repeal of the Townshend duties. Three of the duties were repealed on grounds that they were "anti-commercial," not that they were constitutionally objectionable, and the fourth duty, the tax on tea, was not repealed but was, in the words of Lord North, "retained," "as a mark of the supremacy of Parliament, and an efficient declaration of their [Parliament's] right to govern the Colonies." The marquis of Rockingham oversimplified the constitutional strategy when complaining that the duty on tea "was left as a pepper-corn, merely for the sake of contest with America." Everyone, including Rockingham, knew that there was legal substance behind the strategy. The tax had been "retained upon tea," Virginia's House of Burgesses explained, "for the avowed purpose of establishing a precedent against us."[46]

By retaining the tax on tea Parliament did more than preserve the "right." It set the stage for an escalation of conflict. The tea tax was eventually reconstructed into the Tea Act of 1773, a new tax with the enticing element of making tea substantially cheaper in the colonies. American whig opposition to that legislation precipitated the Boston Tea Party and Parliament found itself trapped by the self-propelling momentum of an unwritten constitution. By enacting the Tea Act, Parliament had pushed the controversy to a point where it had to respond to the Boston Tea Party or jeopardize the claim—legislative supremacy over the colonies—that it had been trying to make with the Tea Act. As one member told the House of Commons, "America does not meet you on the mode of taxation, but upon the question of right." Parliament had to respond or diminish the right.[47]

When Parliament met to consider the Boston Tea Party members wondered whether the Tea Act, promulgated largely to preserve the right to supremacy, was a proper issue with which to force the colonies to acknowledge the right. "Why keep up this duty?" Thomas Townshend, Jr., asked. "Merely to show you ought to keep up the subject of contest," he answered. "The Stamp Act might have been worth preserving, but this is an unproducing tax and nothing but a matter of contest." General John Burgoyne, soon to be posted to the army sent to intimidate the whigs of Boston, argued that the Tea Act could not be repealed precisely because it had been promulgated for contest. "I am sure the tax is not the grievance but the power of laying it," he told the Commons. Burgoyne meant that once the Tea Act had been passed as a test, it had to be supported. "Can you give up the tax, without [giving up] the constitution?" Lord George Germain asked, summing up the predictament into which Parliament had gotten itself with the Tea Act. The constitutional principle at stake was no longer the authority to tax but legislative sovereignty over the colonies.[48]

CHAPTER FOUR

THE AUTHORITY TO REGULATE

American whigs had a solution to the controversy over Parliament's claim to authority to legislate for the colonies in all cases whatsoever. That solution was totally constitutional, turning entirely on legal principles and ignoring America's economic interests or the commercial well being of the colonists. The solution was stated many times, from the beginning of the constitutional crisis until the very end, but its financial implications were never more clearly delineated than by a convention of Pennsylvania counties framing issues to be addressed by the first Continental Congress. There were two aspects of Parliament's authority to legislate that the Congress was expected to resolve: "The *assumed* parliamentary power of *internal* legislation, and the power of regulating trade, as of late exercised." On the second matter, Pennsylvania's delegates were to have the Continental Congress tell Parliament that if Great Britain would renounce all unconstitutional power, the colonies would continue to obey Parliament's constitutional authority. That would mean, the Pennsylvania instructions explained, a continuation of customary constitutional practice with the mother country not only reaping the economic benefits but having unilateral authority to determine what benefits she received and their scope. "From *her* alone we shall continue to receive manufactures; to *her alone* we shall continue to carry the vast multitude of enumerated articles of commerce, the exportation of which her

73

policy has thought fit to confine to herself. With such parts of the world only as *she* has appointed us to deal, we shall continue to deal; and such commodities only as *she* has permitted us to bring from them, we shall continue to bring."[1]

By the premises of economic determinists the Pennsylvanians were conceding to Parliament the pivotal issue of the dispute with the mother country. Yet what they said was mainstream American thought, endorsed by all whigs. "It has not been made a question, that I know of, whether the parliament hath a right to make laws for the regulation of the trade of the colonies," Samuel Adams wrote in the *Boston Gazette* at the relatively late date of January, 1772. Adams further volunteered that in addition to *not questioning* parliamentary authority, colonial whigs positively *acknowledged* Parliament's authority to regulate the foreign trade of the colonies. "*Power* she undoubtedly has to enforce her acts of trade," Adams said of Parliament. Heed well the identity of the person who wrote these words. It is one of those situations where the messenger becomes more important than the message. Adams is generally depicted as the most militant of whigs, an advocate for independence, not a constitutionalist willing to concede Britain its customary perquisites. Yet on the matter of trade regulation, a potential area of contention that some students surmise must have been the *real* cause of the American Revolution, Adams did not question Parliament's "right to make laws for the regulation of the trade of the colonies." Like all other American whigs, he acknowledged that Parliament's authority to regulate the trade of the colonies was constitutional. It is perhaps the most constitutionally revealing concession that could have been made. After all, trade regulation, as Albert B. Southwick has pointed out, was a power every colonial whig knew could have "proved more onerous than a hundred Stamp Acts. This is something to remember by those who hold that the Revolution was ignited by grievances basically and principally economic, and who believe that the political theories advanced were merely so much specious rationalization designed to conceal the 'real' motivations of the struggle."[2]

American whigs fully understood that they could have been conceding the economic store to save the constitutional connection. Consider two pronouncements of the New York General Assembly. "The Authority of the Parliament of *Great-Britain*, to model the Trade of the whole Empire, so as to subserve the Interest of her own, we are ready to recognize in the most intensive and positive Terms," the Assembly assured the House of Commons in October, 1764. "[W]e acknowledge the parliament of Great-Britain [is] necessarily entitled to a supreme direction and government over the whole empire," the New Yorkers repeated in March, 1775. "Their [Parliament's] authority to regulate the trade of the colonies so as to make it subservient to the interest of the mother-country, and to prevent its being injurious to the other parts of his Majesty's dominions, has ever been fully recognized." Once again we are seeing a rule of constitutional law that American whigs were following, not inventing. William Petyt's contention in 1690 that, "The *Parliament of England* cannot bind *Ireland*, as to their Lands, as they have a *Parliament* there: but they may bind them, as to Things transitory, as the shipping of Wool, or Merchandize, to the intent to carry it to another Place beyond the Sea," was, in constitutional substance, the same argument the colonists would be making eighty-five years later.[3]

There was no dispute that Parliament could regulate the trade of the colonies. There were not even disagreements about various meanings of the word "trade." What was disputed was why London had this authority. The theory explaining Parliament's jurisdiction to regulate colonial trade required more precision of definition than any other issue dividing American whigs from imperialists in the 1770s. Unlike much of eighteenth-century constitutional law, it could not be left ambiguous. After the Stamp Act crisis thrust the issue of Parliament's supremacy upon them, it was no longer possible for the colonists to permit the authority to be explained by changing circumstances, to suffer, as a New York pamphlet said in 1765, "the Expediency of the Measure [regulation], to prevent their examining into it's Legality." The theory of regulation just simply could not remain indeterminate as it had been before 1766. Passage of the Declaratory Act required its reformulation to take into account Parliament's claim to legislate in all cases whatsoever. "The difficulty," James Duane told his fellow delegates to the first Continental Congress, "is to establish a Principle upon which we can submit this Authority to Parliament without the Danger of a hurtful Precedent their pleading a Right *to bind in all Cases* whatsoever." To understand how important this question was to colonial whigs consider that had the question been resolved and the colonies not rebelled, the resolution of the matter would have been the most important constitutional event of the eighteenth century.[4]

The caution with which colonial whigs approached the issue is indicative of how seriously it was regarded.[5] The problem they faced was one of constitutional theory, not of commercial practice. It would not be solved by saying that intra-empire and foreign trade could be regulated by Parliament, but not intra-colonial trade. The challenge was not to set limits on the meaning of "trade," but to set limits on the constitutionality of legislation. Needed was a jurisdictional theory explaining two rules of imperial constitutional law. The theory first had to explain why Parliament had jurisdiction over the regulation of colonial trade, and yet did not possess authority to tax Americans for purpose of revenue or to bind the colonies in all cases whatsoever. Second, it had to clarify why the statutes that Parliament had enacted to regulate the trade of the colonies were precedents only for the authority to regulate imperial trade and were not precedents for Parliament's right to pass legislation binding the colonies in matters unrelated to the regulation of trade.

The challenge for American whigs was to devise a formula of indirect consent—not virtual consent, but an indirect consent, either expressed or implied, arising from their free, voluntary will. What disagreement existed was not over the need for colonial consent, but the nature and the form of that consent. To understand the constitutional issue as it was debated and resolved at the first Continental Congress, it is only necessary to consider the arguments of a so-called "conservative" member who is said by some twentieth-century writers to have wanted Congress to concede to Parliament the authority to regulate trade. The constitutional theory of the majority need not be scrutinized as closely. The final resolution of the debate tells the story of what constitutional rule they could live with.

James Duane of New York is our conservative. "I think," John Adams quotes him as saying, "Justice requires that we should expressly ceed to Parliament the Right of regulating Trade." That statement is about as strong a concession as could be made, but we may wonder if it correctly reflects what Duane said. We have his notes for the speech he intended to give on the subject and he took the problem of regulation so seriously that he wrote and rewrote that part of the talk at least four times. The constitutional principle remained unchanged in the various versions. Duane made two points of law. First, he reiterated the familiar legal theory explaining how Parliament's authority was derived from contract. All of the colonies "have submitted to and acquiesced in its Authority for more than a Century," he asserted. "By all therefore the Regulation of Trade may be yielded to Parliament upon the footing of a Compact, reasonable in itself, & essential to the well-being of the whole Empire, as a Commercial People." Second, Duane explained the constitutional doctrine that followed from the implied contract—which, it should be noted, was implied not from parliamentary legislation but from American acceptance, a theory of parliamentary jurisdiction derived from colonial "acknowledgment." It was from "the Spirit of this Compact," as well as "the Necessity of a Supreme controuling Power," and "for the Protection which we have enjoyed & still derive from Great Britain," that Duane would have had the Continental Congress resolve that "we cheerfully acknowledge that it belongs only to Parliament to direct & superintend the Trade of all his Majesty's Dominions. And that this Authority exercised bona fide for the Purposes of securing the Commercial Advantages of the whole Empire to Great Britain with a just Regard to the Interests of its respective Members ought not to be drawn into Question."[6] A month later Duane again raised in Congress the question of the "right of regulating trade," saying, among other arguments, that, "It is agreed on all hands that there must be some supreme controlling power over our trade, and that this can only rest with Parliament." He also made a statement that greatly disturbed John Adams. "Mr. Duane has had his Heart set upon asserting . . . the Authority of Parliament to regulate the Trade of the Colonies," Adams complained. "He is for grounding it on Compact, Acquiescence, Necessity, Protection, not merely on our Consent."[7]

The debate in Congress must have turned on some very fine legal points if Adams could draw a distinction between "compact" and "acquiescence," as Duane used those terms, and the concept of "consent." "Necessity" and "protection" were admittedly risky grounds for the colonists to concede, but in Duane's presentation they were used primarily to explain both the framing of the contract and why there had been a willingness to "acknowledge" the jurisdiction.

Certainly Duane went further than other American whigs thought safe when he reinforced his notion of "Compact" with "the Necessity of a Supreme controuling Power." And, of course, his notion that custom could be proven by showing acceptance of parliamentary statutes made Adams uneasy, even though Duane meant voluntary colonial acceptance. But his formulation of the constitutional basis for Parliament's authority to regulate trade—"we cheerfully acknowledge that it belongs only to Parliament"—does not differ substantially from the resolution adopted the next day by the Continental Congress and generally credited to John Adams. That resolution became part of Proposition Four of the Declaration of Rights of 14 October 1774, the most important part of the most important document promulgated by the first Continental Congress. For American whigs, acceptance by Parliament of Proposition Four was a prime condition for remaining under British rule, for it resolved the only outstanding constitutional question concerning the authority of Parliament to regulate imperial trade. That question had never been whether Parliament could regulate trade, but why.

> [F]rom the necessity of the case, and a regard to the mutual interests of both countries, we cheerfully consent to the operation of such acts of the British parliament, as are bona fide, restrained to the regulation of our external commerce, for the purpose of securing the commercial advantages of the whole empire to the mother country, and the commercial benefits of its respective members, excluding every idea of taxation, internal or external, for raising a revenue on the subjects in America without their consent.

The main difference between this acknowledgment and those of the "conservatives" such as Duane, is that Parliament's jurisdiction was limited to "our external commerce." In the future the imperial legislature would not have jurisdiction over intercolonial or intracolonial trade, a restriction that the British thought a constitutional innovation, but American whigs professed to believe had always been the constitutional rule.[8]

Proposition Four cast American constitutional law in stone. Once Congress formulated the American answer to why Parliament possessed jurisdiction to regulate trade there was a revealed gulf between British constitutional law and colonial whig constitutional theory. The British said that Parliament's authority, even if never exercised, was inherent. American whigs said it was delegated. The distinction between these two doctrines is placed in constitutional context by considering Henry Seymour Conway's plan for peace between Great Britain and the colonies. Conway introduced in the House of Commons a bill that, if enacted, would have promulgated the constitutional proposition that the colonies possessed autonomous legislature authority over their own affairs, "the Legislature of Great Britain reserving only to itself" certain authority including "the due regulation of the trade." Conway thought he was codifying colonial whig constitutional theory, but in fact he was proceeding from British constitutional premises. Under his formulation Parliament possessed the inherent sovereignty and it, the sovereign, did the delegating or granting, in this case by "reserving" a part of its sovereignty. The American rule was the exact opposite. Colonial whigs, knowing that what one sovereign Parliament delegated another sovereign Parliament could reclaim, insisted that the act of delegating, or— their words—of "cheerfully consenting," inherently belonged to the colonies.[9]

We must keep in mind that American whigs argued the fine distinction between James Duane's "cheerfully acknowledge" and John Adams's "cheerfully consent" because they wished to remain in the British empire. They could remain in the empire if Parliament regulated their trade by the authority of their own cheerful consent. They could do so only under constitutional anxiety if Parliament regulated their trade by authority of inherent sovereignty. "Zealous on our part for an indissoluble union with the parent-state," New York's Committee of Correspondence told the lord mayor, aldermen, and Common Council of London less than a month after the battle of Lexington, "studious to promote the glory and happiness of the empire, impressed with a just sense of the necessity of a controuling authority to regulate and harmonize the discordant commercial interests of the various parts, we chearfully submit to a regulation of commerce, by the legislature of the parent-state, excluding, in its nature, every idea of taxation." The Londoners did not need to be told this. They understood the constitutional issue at stake. Twenty-four days earlier they had pleaded the American constitutional case with their king. "Subordinate in commerce, under which the colonies have always chearfully acquiesced, is, they conceive, all that this country ought in justice to require," the London officials petitioned George III, indicating that the words "cheerfully acquiesce" were as much British constitutional words as American constitutional words.[10]

From one perspective Proposition Four was a defeat for American whigs. They had hoped they would never have to consider it. That had been one of the purposes of their strategy of avoidance—not only to avoid giving London precedents of parliamentary supremacy, but also to avoid declarations of ultimate constitutional principle which, just by being ultimate, would drive the British to principles equally extreme. This side of the strategy of avoidance has been missed by most discussions of the American Revolution. There was a time when some scholars of the "progressive school"—or what, in the present context, might be labelled the "anti-ideological school" of history—wrapped their accounts of Parliament's claim of legislative sovereignty around a supposed fact and a historical theme, both of which tended to muddle the story. The supposed fact was that the American case against parliamentary supremacy was "inconsistent." The historical theme was that the inconsistencies in the American case proved colonial whigs insincere when saying the reason for opposing Parliament's authority to legislate was to defend constitutional principles. The theme may no longer be espoused, and the question whether the American case was "inconsistent" no longer interests historians, yet it is worth looking back to the "progressive historians." Their charge of colonial whig inconsistency provides a revealing perspective from which to summarize both the debate over Parliament's authority to legislate and the American strategy of constitutional avoidance.

How, scholars of the progressive school asked, could the colonial whigs have been sincerely defending constitutional rights when the constitutional case they expounded was inherently inconsistent and their constitutional demands changed "from day to day?" It is interesting that all of the "inconsistencies" perceived by the progressives had also been marked by eighteenth-century defenders of Parliament's supremacy: that American legal theory shifted from constitutional law, to natural law, to the rights of man, and "back again"; that colonial whigs "enlarged" the revolutionary controversy from opposition only to internal taxation to demands for independence from Parliament; and that they claimed rights under the British constitution yet rejected dependence under Parliament which that constitution made supreme—positions so inconsistent that they could not have been sincerely asserted. The most important charge, the one scholars of the progressive school found especially convincing, was that American whigs had been constitutional hypocrites, that either they "shifted and advanced the ground of their claim of rights" as the British government reacted to their provocations, or no sooner did they win one concession from the British than they stated a new demand.

The charge of inconsistency was once a dominant thesis in the writing of the history of the American Revolution, at least until Edmund S. Morgan labelled it "a Tory libel that has too readily been accepted by modern historians." As Professor Morgan pointed out, scholars such as Lawrence H. Gipson have "tended to accept the Tory analysis" of the American constitutional defense against parliamentary supremacy. "In objecting to Parliamentary taxation, the Americans talked much about constitutional principles; but the sincerity of their attachment to those principles, Professor Gipson suggests, may be questioned, especially in the light of their shifting from one argument to another as the situation altered." To refute the historical conclusion, Morgan wrote the best concise summary of the evidence upon which it was based.

> [T]he colonists did not really mean what they said. What they wanted was to avoid being taxed, and they had improvised one set of high-sounding principles after another to block the efforts of the British Parliament, to make them pay. When Parliament passed the Stamp Act . . . the colonists invented a distinction between external taxes, which were allowable, and internal taxes, which were not. When Parliament obliged them by repealing the Stamp Act and giving them some external taxes in the Townshend duties, they decided Parliament could tax only for the regulation of trade, not for revenue. When Parliament repealed most of the Townshend duties, but then passed the Coercive Acts to punish Massachusetts for the Boston Tea Party, the colonists decided that Parliament had no authority over them at all, that their only connection with England lay in their loyalty to the king. And they finally repudiated that too in the Declaration of Independence.[11]

It should puzzle us why these shifting principles and doctrines have been said to prove that the American revolutionary controversy was not constitutional. The best explanation seems to be that some twentieth-century scholars have peculiar notions about law and assume that constitutional arguments should proceed to a conclusion by "logical" reasoning rather than legal reasoning. "Of all arguments, a constitutional one requires logic and consistency," Carl N. Degler has suggested, "if it can be shown that an argument used in one place is forgotten in another, then suspicion grows that the constitutional objection is simply a cover for a deeper and more self-interested objection." We may understand why Degler wrote what he did, yet wonder if his conclusion is quite what he intended. As he was addressing historians, it is possible that he was referring to a special kind of suspicion—a historian's suspicion, perhaps. Certainly, it is not a lawyer's suspicion. Lawyers are not troubled if a constitutional argument used in one context is forgotten in the next, unless, of course, they catch an opponent doing the forgetting. Professor Degler's argument is, however, useful for illustrating why the American whig constitutional case against Parliament's authority to legislate for the colonies in all cases whatsoever has been so often dismissed as not constitutional. When commenting on historians who had pointed out that the American pamphleteers shifted their constitutional ground as British actions changed in response to colonial objections, Degler drew from them the conclusion that "[s]uch a procedure certainly belied the colonists' concern for constitutional scruples." Or, as Bernard Bailyn explained the same conclusion, "There was no logic or law behind such gyrations."[12] This perception of illogic or inconsistency caused the progressive historians to ask the wrong question.

Edmund S. Morgan phrased the question that the progressive historians asked: "If the American colonists were sincere, we say, why did they not state at the outset exactly what they believed and then stick to it without faltering?" The question is best understood by again comparing professions, for this is an academic's question, not a lawyer's question. Indeed, in the fact that it is not a lawyer's question can be found its answer. For the answer is not one of those that have been suggested: that the colonial whigs were merely human or that they were motivated by "the desire not to give offense, to show good will and common sense by conceding something in order to retain the rest."[13] The better explanation is that if the American constitutional case was sincere, it would have been argued by the premises of constitutional advocacy. And that is just how it was argued, for had the whigs been eighteenth-century common lawyers, thinking as eighteenth-century common lawyers thought, they would have argued their case exactly as they did argue it.

Take the charge levelled in Morgan's rephrased question: That had American whigs in 1774 been sincere that Parliament could not constitutionally bind them by internal legislation not related to the regulated of trade, they would have pleaded that defense at the very start of the controversy, during the Stamp Act crisis. Of course, American whigs could have opposed the Stamp Act by raising the ultimate issue of the authority of Parliament to legislate for them in all cases whatsoever. Had they done so, they might have met some twentieth-century test for "logic" or "consistency," but they would not have been competent eighteenth-century lawyers. The constitutional issue in 1765 was neither Parliament's authority to legislate nor its authority to impose taxes incidental to the regulation of trade. The issue was the constitutionality of a tax innovation, of the abrogation of precedents with which American had long associated constitutional security, which was why the whigs used the adjective "internal." In the context of eighteenth-century constitutional advocacy, to call the stamp tax "internal" was to focus on the legal contention that the tax was an innovation that departed from long-standing constitutional precedent. It supplemented, therefore, the related grievance that the Stamp Act was taxation without consent. Whigs were not claiming that the tax was illegal, but that as taxation without consent it was unconstitutional and, as internal taxation of the colonies, it was constitutionally unprecedented.

It is a relevant question whether those who have charged that the American whig constitutional case was not "consistent" took common-law methodology into account. Contrary to the assumption made by Professor Degler, a trial or appellate advocate does not seek the widest possible ground on which to stand. The forensic advocate takes a position that is both narrow enough to defend successfully and broad enough to win the point at bar. Put another way, lawyers or other constitutionalists involved in a controversy are not theorists or philosophers. They are advocates. They are not concerned with developing constitutional consistency; their task is to win the case in controversy. They will not adopt an argument they know is "right" but has been rejected by or is likely to antagonize the tribunal of judgment. Whig lawyers of 1765 might or might not have agreed with Professor Gipson that potentially the ultimate issue between the colonies and the mother country was parliamentary sovereignty. But, unlike Gipson, they were disputing a point of law and politics, the constitutionality of the Stamp Act, and their case had to be won in Parliament. If those lawyers wanted the colonies to remain legislatively autonomous parts of the British empire—and the people writing resolutions against the Stamp Act sought to return constitutional affairs to what they had been before the Act—it was not relevant to tell Parliament it was neither supreme nor sovereign. The far better strategy was to do what they did do—concentrate on the fact that any tax on the colonies for purpose of revenue was unprecedented legislation and the fact that the Stamp Act itself violated one of the most fundamental doctrines of English and British constitutional law, that consent of the taxed was required for taxation to be constitutional. These were the probative issues, the two points American lawyers would have concentrated on had they been able to challenge the constitutionality of the Stamp Act in a supreme imperial court with power of judicial review.

Perhaps the "progressive historians" were misled as much by looking in the wrong direction as by asking the wrong questions. Their attention focused on American inconsistencies when American consistencies would have told a more revealing story. Overlooked, as a result, was how consistently colonial whigs maintained their strategy of avoidance, of staying joinder or "maturity" of issue, in hopes that the ultimate question of sovereignty would not be reached. Further instances of their avoidance strategy were set in motion by Parliament's joint resolution urging George III to activate the statute of 35 Henry VIII and the act to suspend the New York General

Assembly. Both were manifestations of internal legislation that colonial whigs held unconstitutional, but, it should be recalled, both were argued in manner to protect the legal rights for which whigs contended without directly disputing the supremacy of Parliament.

Consider the resolution first. Colonial assemblies strongly and frequently protested it but always on theoretical legal grounds of inapplicability or on abstract constitutional grounds. Indeed, protests were so constitutionally circumspect that some assemblies even made the unusual and questionable argument that transportation "beyond the Sea, to be tried, is highly derogatory to the Rights of *British* Subjects"—unusual because Americans almost never claimed British rights, but instead they claimed English rights, and questionable because trial at the venue was not a British right.[14] It was a basic English right that in certain circumstances had been denied to Scots, Welsh, and Irish. The whigs never had to raise their protest against 35 Henry VIII above the theoretical, however, because it was not enforced in the colonies, in part because whig defensive measures prevented enforcement, as when British officials were intimidated by the knowledge that arresting Americans for trial beyond the venue made them liable to tort actions or criminal charges before whig juries in local colonial courts.

An even clearer campaign of avoiding the ultimate constitutional issue was directed against the Mutiny Act commanding American assemblies to provide fuel and other specified provisions for British troops stationed within a colony. One does not have to be an eighteenth-century lawyer to recognize that the tactics of the colonial legislatures—giving London some response that the ministry could tolerate as less than disobedience, yet not quite compliance and certainly not a precedent that Parliament sought—were the tactics of constitutional avoidance. Certainly this was the legal strategy adopted by New York whigs after Parliament retaliated by suspending that colony's General Assembly until it conformed to Parliament's command and furnished all items specified in the Mutiny Act. For the first time in the revolutionary controversy, American whigs were potentially faced with the naked issue of executed parliamentary sovereignty. Had they wished national independence or economic autonomy, they could have joined the issue by challenging the authority of Parliament to order a colonial government to enact specific legislation. But if they wanted what they said they wanted, only their customary constitutional privileges, they would have avoided a confrontation, just as they had with the Stamp Act, the Declaratory Act, and the Townshend duties. That was the strategy adopted by the New York General Assembly at a moment when military circumstances were such that imperial representatives had to take noncompliance as compliance. The whig constitutional objective, after all, had not been to avoid paying for the troops. It had been to avoid giving the British a precedent of parliamentary

sovereignty, and technically they succeeded. We may find the solution con-
trived and unconvincing, but there were sound legal reasons why it was
appealing to lawyers and other constitutionalists who were trying to remain
within the constitutional system.

It would be difficult to exaggerate the importance to colonial whigs of the
strategy of avoiding constitutional precedent or the extent to which they put
the strategy into practice. It was to avoid precedents that crowds took over
colonial streets in 1765 to prevent implementation of the stamp tax, denying
the British a precedent for the authority to tax for purpose of raising revenue. And it was to avoid even the appearance of precedents that colonial
assemblies forbade their London agents to ask for repeal of the Townshend
duties on grounds of expediency even though Lord Hillsborough seemed
to assure them that if they would plead inexpediency the taxes would be
repealed. A petition asserting that Parliament had enacted inexpedient legislation was not constitutionally harmless. A later minister might say that just
by asking that the law be repealed the petitioning colony had acknowledged
Parliament's authority to legislate.

The conclusion may be understated. It is not necessary to contend that
the motivations of colonial whigs were solely constitutional. All that is claimed
is that their constitutional strategies were consistently forensic. The purpose
behind the strategies is a question quite separate from whether the strategies were dictated by legal considerations. Nor is it denied that there are
different perspectives from which to evaluate events. Even if we insist on
remaining "progressive historians" or economic determinists, however, we
should not forget that eighteenth-century lawyers argued as they were trained
to argue, like eighteenth-century lawyers, and that in the eighteenth century
it was usual for political arguments to cite precedent, draw analogy, and
appeal to doctrine, a methodology that in the twentieth century is more
likely to be confined to appellate advocacy. If we view the constitutional
controversy from that perspective, the perspective of forensic advocacy and
the common-law mind, we should understand why the "inconsistencies" in
the American whig case have been reassessed in our own times. Indeed, the
"inconsistency" of the changes in argument once cited as proof that the
colonial case could not have been constitutional turns out to be convincing
evidence of how very constitutional the whig case actually was. Of course,
the legal strategy pursued by the imperial side of the controversy was also
constitutionally consistent. Tragically for the old British empire, however, it
was not a strategy of constitutional avoidance. It was, rather, a strategy of
sovereign command, a British adoption of the principle of legislative sovereignty and a British abrogation of the English constitutional principle that
Americans cherished above all others, the rule of law.

CHAPTER FIVE

THE AUTHORITY OF
THE PREROGATIVE

Avoidance of constitutional confrontation with the mother country continued to guide American whig constitutional strategy until 1773 when circumstances in Boston forced the colonists to choose between avoiding giving Parliament a precedent of supremacy or avoiding a confrontation over the Tea Act. Providing a striking instance of the importance they attached to the forms of law, the whig leaders of Massachusetts chose to avoid the precedent. Of the five statutes asserting parliamentary power outlined in the last chapter, the Tea Act of 1773 was the one least directly concerned with legislating supremacy. It was, however, the most memorable as it was the law that forced American whigs to choose between avoiding a precedent of taxation or avoiding a constitutional confrontation. The American choice—to avoid the precedent—drove Parliament to enact another series of laws raising the claim of supremacy to such a level whigs could no longer maneuver around the issue and Great Britain could no longer retreat.

Constitutional strategy was not the overt purpose of the Tea Act. Finances were—the finances of the East India Company. "[T]he East India Company have now actually in their warehouse very near seventeen million pounds of tea, which the Company report near three years' consumption," Frederick North, Lord North explained in the House of Commons. "It must be obvious to everybody to what a great loss the East India Company keep it in

85

their warehouses." Americans were a major cause of the surplus. Protesting the tea tax, the last of the Townshend duties, they had been boycotting tea imported from Britain. To reduce inventory, North proposed lowering from one shilling to three pence the tax on each pound of tea exported to America. Some members of Parliament warned the ministry that the entire duty had to be removed or Americans would still refuse to accept the tea. But North had more in mind: he wanted revenue from the sale of the tea to resurrect the Townshend Acts' abortive constitutional program of paying officials' salaries then being paid by colonial assemblies. "If the East India Company will export tea to America," he insisted, it would "very much facilitate carrying on government in that part." From the perspective of constitutional law North was saying that the constitutional issue had not changed, that the Tea Act was as much supremacy legislation as the Townshend Acts had been. For American whigs, therefore, the impost on tea was as constitutionally offensive in its new guise as a single tax as it had been as part of the Townshend package.[1]

It is hard to believe but some members of Parliament were surprised by American reaction to the Tea Act. "Whoever can sell the cheapest, the American will buy," one confidently predicted. "Tea may be exported cheap enough to find a market in America, and preserve the duty," Lord North agreed. "You will have your market and your revenue." Surely it was to be expected that this "3d duty can never be the bone of contention, especially when it is consumed 9d per lb. cheaper than formerly." North may not have understood American constitutional commitment but he understood the constitutional issue. As every member of Parliament realized, North's legislative purpose for enacting the Tea Act had been both to save and to force the constitutional issue. Edmund Burke is but one example. Speaking on the very day that war broke out across the Atlantic at Lexington and Concord, he reminded the ministry that "the 3d duty" may have been "given up as a tax of revenue," but it had been retained "for a tax of litigation and quarrell. The 3d is not the object; it's the principle that the Americans could not submit to; they would be slaves if they did." After all, as Charles James Fox told the Commons that same day, "[a] tax can only be laid for three purposes; the first for a commercial regulation, the second for a revenue, and the third for asserting your right."[2]

At first glance, the American reaction to the Tea Act—the Boston Tea Party—looks like a change in whig strategy from the policy of avoiding acknowledgment of Parliament's right or avoiding colonial claims of legislative autonomy, to direct confrontation and open violence. That impression would be wrong. In point of constitutional fact, American whigs tried to continue their practice of avoidance. The best reading of the evidence is that the whig leadership, even in Boston, hoped to repeat the legal tactics that had worked successfully during the Stamp Act crisis. As in 1765, when whig crowds took to colonial streets to prevent implementation of the stamp tax, denying the British a precedent for the authority to tax for purposes of revenue, so, in 1774, did crowds in Boston and all other colonial seaports except Charleston, South Carolina, prevent tea from even staying aboard ships at anchor for more than twenty days. By implication if not explicitly, that time limit had been set by parliamentary legislation. Once a ship carrying tea arrived in a colonial port, that tea was imported and had to be entered at the customs house as a dutied product. After twenty days, if the tea was not unladed and the provisions of law met, the tea was seized, sold, and the proceeds applied to satisfy the duty. Either directly or indirectly, once a ship was in harbor, London would obtain a precedent of colonial payment of the tax on tea. Moreover, once in a harbor, a ship bearing tea could not depart without a clearance from the customs house, a pass from the naval officer, or (at least in the case of Boston) a pass from the governor. To further complicate the situation, there were people in Boston, including Governor Thomas Hutchinson and the whig selectmen, who interpreted seventeenth-century statutes as providing that no tea, once exported from England, could be reentered there on pain of confiscation.

Why Parliament mandated these restrictions is unclear. Although unlikely, it is not impossible that the ministry was trying to obtain the precedent for taxation that had eluded London when the Stamp Act and the Townshend duties were repealed. The whigs still could have avoided the precedent without overt, direct disobedience had the first tea ship, *Dartmouth*, remained outside the legal limits of the harbor as it was warned to do by both the town meeting and Hutchinson. That was how the problem was solved in most other ports. The pilots anchored the ships outside the harbors of New York and Philadelphia, and the whigs of those towns did not have to throw tea overboard. Boston whigs apparently formed the same plan but had to abandon it when *Dartmouth* made an entry, perhaps because her owner hoped to earn freight on the remainder of the cargo, which he would have lost had the ship not come in.

After the whig crowd prevented the owner from unlading, he applied to Hutchinson for a pass permitting him to depart from the harbor. Pleading lack of authority, the governor refused. *Dartmouth* could neither unlade nor leave port. Both sides of the constitutional controversy, imperial governor and colonial town meeting, seemed to be trapped by parliamentary law. On 17 December 1773, after *Dartmouth* had been in harbor for twenty days, the tea would, by law, be entered at the customs house and, even if none were sold, London would have its precedent because the duty would be credited on entry. That was why Boston's whigs staged their Tea Party on the night of the sixteenth. The law, and perhaps Thomas Hutchinson, had left them no other way to avoid the precedent. Hutchinson admitted that their object had been avoidance, not destruction, when he wrote his predecessor as governor that Boston whigs, after they "had tried every method they could think of to force the tea back to England, and all in vain, they . . . reassembled at Giffin's Wharf, and in two or three hours destroyed three hundred and forty chests." Again we have a statement that is more important for the writer than for what was written. Here is the royal governor, the official most responsible for upholding the authority of Parliament in Massachusetts Bay, admitting that the Bostonians wanted to avoid the Tea Party and that the whigs changed their legal tactics because all their options of avoidance had been blocked by the circumscriptive rules of imperial legislation.[3]

Of course it can be said, as scholars often say, that law was not a factor in the Boston Tea Party, that the whig leadership felt it was time to take the conflict to violence and the arrival of the duticd tea was a handy excuse for starting civil war. After all, the Americans could have let the tea be landed, refused to buy it, and have said that the duty entered was not a precedent for a colonial tax because it had been paid by consignees of the East India Company or paid by pro-imperialists at the public sale conducted by the customs house. True, the British would have claimed the precedent, saying that what mattered was that the tax had been paid by Americans, but, at best, it would have been a tarnished precedent.

Even from the perspective of law, an argument can be made that the Tea Party was not necessary. Had the tea been entered as duticd goods, the precedent would have been so weak that the constitutional relationship of the colonists to Parliament would not have been altered. But Lord North did not intend to argue the precedent as law before a judicial tribunal. Its value to the ministry was more political than legal—in parliamentary debates and as precedential evidence to persuade the British public that the American constitutional argument was wrong. Perhaps the best explanation is that American whigs had come to the conclusion that, with the Tea Act, the administration had pushed its program of legislating supremacy so far that any possible acquiescence, even a badly tarnished precedent, had to be avoided.

The Boston Tea Party caused an even greater sensation in the mother country than had the Stamp Act riots. "There never was, since the [Glorious] *Revolution*, so important a crisis in the constitution of this country," a London newspaper told its readers. Even the opposition in Parliament agreed that Boston had to be disciplined. There was, in fact, little argument about the need of hitting the town with a bill of pains and penalties. The debate was over the nature of the punishment and its severity.[4]

The bill of pains and penalties—actually a parliamentary statute—withdrew from Boston "the officers of his Majesty's customs," and made it unlawful to unladen or to load nonmilitary goods in Boston harbor. The port was to be closed to all civilian traffic "until it shall sufficiently appear to his Majesty that full satisfaction has been made by or on behalf of the inhabitants of the said town of *Boston*" to the East India Company for the teas destroyed in the Tea Party. This legislation is known as the Boston Port Act and everyone understood its purpose was not so much to punish Boston as to assert parliamentary supremacy over the colonies. "It is to tell America," Lord North assured the House of Commons, "that you are in earnest, if we do not mean totally to give up the matter in question. We must assert our right at this time, while . . . it is in our power."[5]

On the whole, the British felt the Boston Port Act mild punishment—appropriately tough and prudent, perhaps, but not unduly severe. The administration thought the legislation so reasonable it would be self-executing, needing at most five frigates and, as Boston would quickly conclude that the East India company had to be paid, the crown would have no difficulty ruling that the harbor could be reopened. A second general assumption was that the other American colonies would not care what Parliament did to Massachusetts Bay, since, in North's words, "[t]he rest of the colonies will not take fire at the proper punishment inflicted on those who have disobeyed your authority . . . if we exert ourselves now with firmness and intrepidity, it is the more likely they will submit to our authority."[6]

Again Lord North depreciated the constitutional aspects of a dispute he hoped was merely political, and, again, he discounted the extent to which principle determined American reaction. The Boston Port Act stunned colonists as much as the Boston Tea Party had stunned London. The merchants and citizens of Boston's rival ports from New York to South Carolina resolved that the Act "is, in the highest degree arbitrary in its principles, oppressive in its operation, unparalleled in its rigour, indefinite in its exactions, and subversive of every idea of *British* liberty." London should not have been surprised by this reaction. Had the ministry given the attention it should have to American attachment to the old constitution of customary restraints, it could have anticipated the support Boston received from the remainder of North America. Colonial whigs, weighing the Boston Port Act from the vantage point of the two eighteenth-century constitutions, especially the potential of the constitution of legislative sovereignty, concluded that "its principle extends to every inch of *English America*." "We had been sitting in Assembly near three weeks," a Virginia burgess wrote a brother in Great Britain, "when a quick arrival from London brought us the Tyrannic Boston Port Bill, no shock of Electricity could more suddenly and universally move—Astonishment, indignation, and concern seized all. The shallow Ministerial device was seen thro instantly, and every one declared . . . that it demanded a firm and determined union of all the Colonies to repel the common danger."[7]

We may be reasonably certain that the Boston Port Act alone was ample constitutional provocation to gather the colonists in a Continental Congress and to start them down the path toward civil war. We will never know for certain, however, for Parliament did not stop with closing New England's main harbor. Four more statutes were rapidly enacted which, together with the Boston Port Act, are known in history as the coercive acts or the intolerable acts. These statutes: 1) altered by parliamentary fiat the charter government of Massachusetts Bay; 2) provided trial outside the venue for British officials accused of committing capital crimes in Massachusetts, thus, in a sense, reversing the procedure of 35 Henry VIII; 3) extended imperial authority to quarter troops in certain types of privately-owned colonial buildings; and 4) limited the government of Quebec to an appointed executive without a representative assembly or elected officials of any kind. Each of these statutes was direct internal legislation, and, seen in the lights of whig jurisprudence, each abrogated in substantive ways the constitutional rights of the American colonists or threatened their constitutional security. From the point of view of whig lawyers and their strategy of avoidance, the coercive acts so substantively changed the constitutional controversy there was little alternative to constitutional resistance.

For the first time Americans were confronted by the ultimate constitutional issue of executed parliamentary sovereignty; confronted, that is, by an exercise of legislative authority that could not be ignored, distinguished away, or neutralized by partial compliance. The resolutions passed by a Rhode Island town meeting tell us what whigs all up and down the Atlantic coast were saying: "That the act of the British Parliament, claiming the right to make laws binding upon the colonies, in all cases whatsoever, is inconsistent with the natural, constitutional and charter rights and privileges of the inhabitants of this colony." At last the Declaratory Act had become an issue in the constitutional controversy. That colonial whigs finally stated the Declaratory Act as *the* grievance does not mean that they had changed their constitutional stand or even that they were inconsistent. Now, after eight years, the Declaratory Act had become the constitutional grievance in law as well as in symbol because, if we think about them as law, the coercive acts were the Declaratory Act promulgated.[8]

It is not enough that we understand the constitutional perspective of the colonists. We must also understand the constitutional perspective of the British government. We can learn much about it by considering a statement recently written explaining British motivations. Generally it is not useful to single out for criticism assertions of history that are obviously false. Occasionally, however, there are claims so erroneous their very restatement serves to clarify the record just by being completely wrong. Our example deals with the authority of Parliament to bind the colonies in all cases whatsoever.

"The British located sovereignty in Parliament," it was claimed, "not because they could not imagine locating it anywhere else, but because they were persuaded that the consequences of doing so would lead to the loss of their claim to control over the colonies."[9]

It would be difficult to formulate another sentence demonstrating a greater misunderstanding of eighteenth-century British constitutional government. The fact is that the British located sovereignty in Parliament not to control the colonies, but to control the king. The colonies were immaterial. Had they been susceptible to control it would not have mattered if they were controlled by the war office, the Board of Trade, or a secretary of state reporting to Parliament. What mattered was that they not be controlled by the crown or that they be associated with the crown independently of Parliament. That was why all the leaders of Parliament, whigs as much as tories, demanded that Americans first acknowledge Parliament's sovereign "right" over the colonies and then Parliament would agree to limit or not to exercise the right.

Parliament was caught in the same uncertainty of British constitutional dynamics in which American whigs were caught. The Americans could not agree to even a *pro forma* acknowledgment of Parliament's right when the current parliament was unable to bind a future parliament and no one could predict if some future parliament might take advantage of the acknowledgement and exercise the right. American liberty required that Parliament first renounce the right and then the colonists could discuss what powers Parliament possessed for the regulation of trade and the general superintendence of the empire. Parliament, however, could not renounce its authority for that would have left the populous, wealthy thirteen colonies constitutionally linked to the crown, independent of Parliament in all matters except the regulation of all foreign and some intra-empire trade. Any revenues or requisitions would have been paid to George III, not as king of Great Britain but as king of Georgia or king of Connecticut.

Once more it is necessary to make what by now is a familiar point. The prerogativism of American whigs was not an intellectual inconsistency forced on them when the Coercive Acts left them nowhere else to turn except to natural law. American monarchism was the logical product of their attachment to the principles of the old English constitution, the proof of their sincerity to constitutionalism. It was not new, but even though muted until 1774, it had always been part of their constitutional solution to the controversy concerning Parliament's authority to legislate in all cases whatsoever, should Great Britain push them that far. It had never been concealed, but had been stated throughout the controversy, and even earlier, as by the Council and House of Burgesses of Virginia, in 1764, before passage of the Stamp Act. In a petition to George III, they implored the king "to protect your People of this Colony in the Enjoyment of their ancient and inestimable Right of being governed by such Laws respecting their internal Polity and Taxation as are derived from their own Consent, with the Approbation of their Sovereign or his Substitute." Ten years later, the Continental Congress made the same constitutional connection. It did not petition Parliament. It did petition the king. "We ask but for peace, liberty, and safety," Congress told George III. "We wish not for a diminuation of the prerogative, nor do we solicit the grant for any new right in our favour. Your royal authority over us and our connexion with Great-Britain, we shall always carefully and zealously endeavour to support and maintain." These three sentences were the most revolutionary statements made by the first Continental Congress. If American whigs were prepared to support what was said, they were risking civil war. The argument was phrased with great care, but no words could soften the constitutional reality. Congress said it did not wish "a diminution of the prerogative," for that was what it meant to say from the American perspective. From the British perspective, however, Congress appeared to be asking an increase of the prerogative, or even a revival of the prerogative. For Congress wanted the king to assume an active role in the imperial constitution. "We therefore most earnestly beseech your majesty," the Congress petitioned, "that your royal authority and interposition may be used for our relief and that a gracious answer may be given to our petition."[10]

The Americans solved the legislative grievance by entrusting all connection between Great Britain and the colonies to the executive branch of the government. "That the executive power," whigs of a North Carolina county explained, "constitutionally vested in the Crown and which presides equally over Great Britain and America, is a sufficient security for the due subordination of the Colonies without the Parliament's assuming powers of Legislation and Taxation which we enjoy distinct from, and in equal degree with them." That statement is what the eighteenth century would have called a "constitutional" resolution to the legislation controversy. All that Parliament had to do was "relinquish all pretence of right to govern the *British* Colonies in *America*, and leave that to whom it solely and exclusively belongs, namely, the King, our lawful Sovereign, with his Parliament in the respective Colonies, and the *Americans* have a Constitution without seeking further." Considered in the perspective of the supremacy controversy, Americans defended the prerogative link not as a change in constitutional law but a restoration of constitutional security. When the Lords and Commons attempted to assert legislative authority over the colonies, they also usurped the position of the king.[11]

The twentieth century may no longer understand what was going on in the 1770s. As Americans understood the constitutional situation, they were not contending for constitutional separation but for restoration of their constitutional connection with the king. They were, in other words, pushing against the republican grain. They wanted the certainty of the restrained, balanced constitution, not experimentation with civic virtue. We see this by considering not what we think they should have wanted, but what they said they sought: a revived monarchy with a king who, in imperial government at least, would again provide balance to the balanced constitution. George III was asked to veto bills by Parliament legislating for the colonies and to prorogue sessions or call elections when Parliament threatened American rights. Unwilling to depend on the shifting sands of natural law or to abandon their claims to rights under the British constitution, American whigs had only one place to turn once the Coercive Acts made it impossible for them to continue their strategy of avoiding the issue of Parliament's right to legislate. They turned to the English constitution, especially to the principles of the seventeenth-century English constitution, that is, to the royal prerogative.

The American whig formulation of a prerogative solution may seem fantastic today. We are told that the colonists espoused something called "republicanism" or, maybe, classical humanism, but never monarchism. Yet if we abandon our own predilections and think instead as English-speaking people thought in the eighteenth century, it will be seen that there was a constitutional logic and a constitutional consistency to the prerogative solution. One graphic piece of evidence is the fact that the same solution by the same logic was being pursued in contemporary Great Britain. Much has been made in recent years of the influence upon American whigs of the so-called "radicals" in eighteenth-century British politics. Their program for government reform was varied, with individual "radicals" reacting to different causes of unhappiness such as bloated bureaucracy, decreasing agrarian influence, or new sources of wealth. What interests us is that the most vocal complaints focused on Parliament, especially on how parliamentary supremacy was being converted into parliamentary sovereignty, a lesson taught in part by the constitutional controversy between Parliament and American whigs. The fact that they, too, asked George III to become an active weight in a balanced constitution is empirical evidence not only that there was legal logic to the prerogative solution, but that it may have been the most persuasive or "constitutional" solution remaining in English-British constitutional law.

If anything, British reformers went further than American whigs. They not only sought resurrection of the royal prerogative, they wanted the House of Commons to resume one of its dormant functions once used to check the prerogative: the power of impeaching royal officials. The prerogative power that the king most frequently was asked to exercise was the veto. Given the conditions of constitutional law in the 1760s and 1770s, however, the most extreme demands were petitions praying King George to dismiss the House of Commons and call new elections. These "radicals" did not seek what today would be called a radical constitution, but only what the eighteenth century would have called a radical remedy for constitutional grievances. They wanted a constitutional shield protecting them from the sovereign supremacy of an unrepresentative, unresponsive Parliament. To obtain it they sought to put checks and balances back into the eighteenth-century constitution by reclaiming the apparatus of the seventeenth-century constitution as it had functioned before the Glorious Revolution diminished the prerogative and anointed Parliament with the potentials of sovereignty. We may suspect they knew it was too late, that the British constitution could no longer contemplate institutional restraints on legislative discretion, but can we be sure?

The quest by British radicals and American whigs for a constitutional check to legislative sovereignty encountered an immovable constitutional obstacle. George III, the constitutional instrument to which they looked for constitutional restoration, was a constitutionalist of parliamentary supremacy not of the constitution of customary, prescriptive rights. "[T]here is a time, when it is morally demonstrable that men cease to be representatives," the lord mayor, aldermen, and livery of London remonstrated, praying the king to dismiss the Commons of 1770 and call new elections. "That time is now arrived. The present House of Commons do not represent the people." We need not consider the arguments. The king was not going to dissolve Parliament no matter what was said. Told that he had a constitutional duty to act, George III implied that his constitutional authority was gone. "I shall always be ready to receive the requests, and to listen to the complaints of my subjects," George told the London officials. But he would do nothing "injurious to my parliament, and irreconcilable to the principles of the constitution." From the perspective of today George III was acting constitutionally, taking the crown out of politics and preparing the way for the responsible government of Parliament and cabinet. "I have ever made the law of the land the rule of my conduct, esteeming it my chief glory to reign over a free people," he explained. "With this view I have always been careful to execute faithfully the trust reposed in me, as to avoid even the appearance of invading any of those powers which the constitution has placed in other hands." We in the twentieth century not only know what the king meant, we approve, for he was moving Great Britain toward today's constitution. It would be well, however, to consider the perspective of those eighteenth-century Americans and Britons apprehensive of Parliament's arbitrary power. George III was saying more to them than that he would keep himself out of politics. He was taking the crown out of government. Constitutional rights would not be protected from the caprice of an arbitrary Parliament, even in theory. The prerogative would no longer enforce the rule of law.[12]

The prerogative solution may have been constitutionally logical under the constitution of customary rights but it was constitutionally impossible under the constitution of sovereign command. From the perspective of British tories as well as British whigs the American colonists were seeking to secure their constitutional liberty at the expense of British constitutional liberty. Recall what was previously said of how the Glorious Revoultion of 1688 had established parliamentary supremacy over the crown. By the 1770s the legacy of the Glorious Revolution had made American liberty the direct institutional opposite of British liberty. For the British, the Glorious Revolution had been the triumph of liberty, a liberty institutionalized in parliamentary sovereignity over the law, the constitution, and the monarchy. For Americans, however, liberty remained what it had been before 1688, the liberty of the constitution protected by the rule of law. It was this dichotomy that Attorney General William DeGray had in mind when he urged members of the House of Commons to praise George III for preserving British liberty. After the king had rejected petitions praying that he dissolve Parliament, DeGrey reminded his colleagues in the Commons of the constitutional necessity to "preserve the independence of our own body, as involving the liberty of the people, and defend it against the people themselves misguided and inflamed by faction and self-interest, with no less activity and perseverance than against the Crown or the Lords." Therefore, he said, the House should praise the king for avoiding constitutional temptation. "Let us," DeGrey urged, "look up with affection and gratitude to the prince, who, knowing the value of our constitution, as well to himself as to his subjects, has nobly rejected an opportunity which the late Petitions have given him, of destroying the equilibrium of the constitution by increasing his own power, which a sovereign less virtuous and less wise would have embraced."[13]

Five years after DeGrey lauded George III for not using "radical" discontent to increase "his own power," members of all factions in both houses of Parliament commended the king for his fidelity to the eighteenth-century constitution by rejecting American petitions praying that he revive seventeenth-century prerogativism. Even the king's first minister, Lord North, said the American war was being fought not just to establish parliamentary supremacy over the colonies, but to defend the constitution against American monarchism. Charles James Fox had irritated North by reminding the Commons of the "political distinctions" between "Whig and Tory," and calling North and the other ministers "tories." "His lordship then said," a London newspaper, quoting Lord North, reported, "that if he understood the meaning of the words Whig and Tory, which the last speaker had mentioned, he conceived that it was the characteristic of whiggism to gain as much for the people as possible, while the aim of toryism was to increase the prerogative. That in the present case, administration contended for the right of Parliament, while the Americans talked of their belonging to the crown. Their language therefore was that of toryism."[14]

Two hundred years of parliamentary supremacy have clouded our hindsight. We cannot take Lord North as seriously as did his contemporaries because we cannot appreciate the degree to which the eighteenth-century British constitutional mind thought that the potential of prerogative power was the ultimate menace to the perfect liberty established at the Glorious Revolution. One possibility was on everyone's mind. Suppose that the colonies and Great Britain were united only by common interest and allegiance to a common king, and that the king was voted revenue directly by his American "Houses of Commons." Some people thought that the reality of the danger was proven by what had happened with the revenues of Ireland. In fact, when Josiah Tucker argued that total American independence, with all connections broken to both crown and Parliament, would strengthen British liberty, other people said Great Britain should also separate from Ireland, "to *preserve our present happy constitution.*" The reason: "Our connections with Ireland invests the king with an amazing degree of power, by giving him the disposal of many places both in church and state; not to mention the pensions which are liberally bestowed to silence the opposers of government in England. It is sufficient to hint at this, to shew how much the constitution will be benefitted by such a separation." People who drafted plans for a continual union between Great Britain and North America under which Parliament would no longer possess authority to legislate for the colonies, generally provided either that requisitions paid the king by the colonies be controlled by Parliament or that revenue raised in one of the dominions for the use of the king could not be remitted or spent in another of the king's dominions.[15]

There is but one final point to be made. The constitutional necessity to check prerogative power shaped the course of the American Revolution controversy much more than has been credited in this century. "Even a Burke, who boasts of his Philanthropy and Love of Liberty, would have bound America to unlimited Subjection," Thomas Northcote wrote the Irish Reform Committee. The fact was not surprising to Northcote in 1783 and it should not be to us living in a different constitutional epoch. It may have been a power Burke would not have exercised, but he, too, would have used the word "unlimited" to describe it. The colonists understood why. British officials made certain of that by frequently telling colonial leaders that their liberty depended on Parliament, not on the king. William Samuel Johnson, writing the governor of Connecticut, used quotation marks to indicate that he was directly quoting the words of the earl of Hillsborough, secretary of state for the colonies. "It is essential to the constitution," Hillsborough told Johnson, "to preserve the supremacy of Parliament inviolate; and tell your friends in America . . . that it is as much their interest to support the constitution and preserve the supremacy of Parliament as it is ours. Neither of us can be safe but upon that ground." That constitutional ground was Parliament's institutional role as a check on royal power.[16]

For us the eighteenth-century need for proportional constitutional structure may appear as an overemphasis on symmetry. For members of Parliament and the educated British public, it was a matter of keeping constitutional liberty in balance. The taught articulation was as familiar among military officers as it was among barristers. "[T]he whole of our political system," General John Burgoyne has been quoted as observing, "depends upon the preservation of its great and essential parts distinctly, and no part is so great and essential as the supremacy of the legislation." Political thought in the second half of the eighteenth century was different than in later centuries. We should not conclude that British leaders thought more narrowly. It was, rather, that they thought more constitutionally.[17]

Charles Howard McIlwain was not sure of the distinction. He believed that British leaders had thought narrowly. In his study, *The American Revolution: A Constitutional Interpretation*, McIlwain concluded that the controversy became too legal, for which he blamed the lawyers. It was the lawyers, he claimed, such as the lord chief justice, the earl of Mansfield, the government's chief legal advisor, who, unable to comprehend the controversy except from the narrowness of law, prevented the administration from seeing that the solution was a commonwealth of independent legislatures joined in union only by a common allegiance to the crown. "The rigorous logic of his theory of sovereignty compelled Mansfield to demand one ultimate and undivided authority and he could brook no exception even of a practical kind," McIlwain wrote, claiming that Mansfield's jurisprudence anticipated that of John Austin who, in 1832 under a much different constitution, taught the following generations of British lawyers not to confuse law with morality. Austin defined "law" as general commands of a superior enforced by sanctions. "But Austinianism is logic, and logic is not all of life," McIlwain complained. "So, happily, an illogical modern Empire has arisen not unlike the modern limited monarchy for the realm itself, in defiance of Austin and in the teeth of Lord John Russell's repetition of Mansfield's dictum: no dependence, no sovereignty; with its futile logic, always so soothing to the timid souls who live in constant dread of surrendering their 'sovereignty' to somebody or other."[18]

McIlwain was right. Mansfield dreaded surrendering sovereignty to somebody. He is wrong, however, to think that somebody was the colonial assemblies. "For Lord Mansfield," McIlwain continued, "the sovereignty of the Parliament and the dependency of the dominions must continue to coexist. They must stand or fall together." John Adams, who believed that colonial assemblies could be autonomous from Parliament yet remain in allegiance to the king, was praised by McIlwain for seeing the practical situation much more clearly than Mansfield, that is, less like a lawyer. "Adams, Austinian though in a certain sense he was, looked further into the future, and saw what Mansfield could not, that for a working empire his theory must be modified in practice by a voluntary concession. Such a compromise, however, was too advanced for the rigorous logic of the eighteenth century."[19]

McIlwain must be approached with caution. His error was not just to be anachronistic; it was also that he professed to be discussing law when in fact he was treating it with contempt. He ignored law when saying that the British Commonwealth of Nations solution to the American Revolution controversy was too "advanced" for the eighteenth century. In terms of law, that solution could have retarded, not advanced, British liberty. It would have been difficult for Lord Mansfield—or any other member of Parliament or lawyer—to have seen the solution "advancing" anything except the autonomy and power of the crown. Keep in mind points just made: that fear of an increase of royal authority saturated the constitutional thinking of that day. There was, for example, much concern over the influence that George III derived from the revenue of Ireland and of the pensions he was able to award on the Irish establishment. "[F]rom the perspective of Britain's own internal constitutional development during the previous century," Jack P. Greene has pointed out, "colonial theories about the organization of the empire seemed dangerously retrograde. By placing the resources of Ireland and the colonies directly in the hands of the Crown and beyond the reach of Parliament, those theories appeared to strike directly at the root of the legislative supremacy that, for them, was the primary legacy of the Glorious Revolution."[20]

Lord Mansfield deserves better than to be tarred with the Austinianism with which Charles Howard McIlwain smeared him. He may have been narrow, but he was narrow on the side of British constitutional liberty, not narrow on the side of denying Americans a premature commonwealth of nations. "I seek for the liberty and constitution of this Kingdom no farther back than the Revolution," Mansfield said, referring to 1688 and the Glorious Revolution. "There I take my stand." He stood there with every other British statesman, lawyer, constitutionalist, and member of Parliament.[21]

Had Lord Mansfield agreed that sovereignty could be divided, and that Parliament could renounce its supremacy over colonial assemblies while Americans remained in allegiance to the king, he risked taking the same constitutional step backwards from the Glorious Revolution that American whigs had already taken. Given the British constitution of 1775 and the legacy of the Glorious Revolution, the choice was not only between the supremacy of Parliament and American legislative autonomy, it was also between the supremacy of Parliament and the king's prerogative. If sovereignty was divided by giving the colonial assemblies supremacy within their jurisdictions, and limiting the imperial jurisdiction of Parliament, a potential sphere of power was created for the king to fill.

It does not do to think of the twentieth century and of Elizabeth II, to say as McIlwain would, that George III could have been the head, the cement, the binding link of empire and nothing else. If it is possible for us to imagine a British commonwealth of nations, it was not possible for Lord Chief Justice Mansfield and his colleagues in the eighteenth-century British government. They could not foresee the twentieth-century commonwealth as easily as McIlwain suggests. George III was the monarch then, not Victoria or George V. The eighteenth-century constitution of 1775 was less than a hundred years removed from the Glorious Revolution and the struggle against the House of Stuart. George III was still a powerful monarch, and he was powerful mainly through the exercise of what was called influence. To have provided him with the leverage of being the link of empire, constitutionally risked the chance that his influence would be increased. The concern was not that his influence would increase in imperial affairs; that was not the risk. The risk was that as a result of his enhanced role in the governance of the empire, his influence in Great Britain would have been increased. It was not until the nineteenth century—after the Reform Act, the final demise of the royal prerogative, with the establishment of what the British refer to as responsible government, with the crown out of politics and a party system selecting the nation's leaders—that dominion status within the empire with allegiance to the queen became constitutionally possible.

It was these constitutional considerations that explain why the controversy became too legal; why the British insisted that the Americans first had to acknowledge "the right" and then there could be a renunciation of "the exercise." If the Americans had acknowledged an abstract supremacy, Parliament could then have devised a constitutional mechanism to check any threat from the crown should the colonies provide the king with revenue. But the Americans could not acknowledge without risking their constitutional security to the whims and changing politics of some future parliament. The controversy, therefore, became too legal not in an abstract sense, but because the procedures or the mechanics of constitutional advocacy provided no opportunity for a political solution unless either the British or the Americans surrendered a constitutional principle they thought essential for their constitutional liberty. The dynamics of the eighteenth-century British constitution had produced a constitutional dilemma. American liberty—the right to be free of arbitrary power—could not be secured under parliamentary supremacy. British liberty—the representative legislature over the crown—could not be secured without parliamentary sovereignty.

CHAPTER SIX

CONCLUSION

Civil war was not inevitable. The constitutional rule that the statutes of one parliament could not bind a future parliament, did not mean there were no solutions. What it meant was that any solution had to be political, not constitutional. The British constitution had brought Americans to a dead end. One reason why the question of Parliament's right to bind the American colonies in all cases whatsoever was resolved on the battlefield of Yorktown was that, under the British constitution, there was no constitutional tribunal except Parliament with jurisdiction to settle it.

The battle of Yorktown presaged a change of form but not a change of substance for American constitutionalism. In one respect, it could be said that American constitution framers repudiated both their English constitutional past and the methodology of the constitution of prescriptive, customary rights when they drafted organic acts and submitted them to the voters for popular approval. In another respect, it could be said that they put the theory of the original contract into practice, that the act of drafting, debating, and adopting a written constitution was contractarianism in action. Some state constitutions said they were contracts, even codifying the contractarian doctrine that government is founded in compact.[a]

---

[a] "That all government of right originates from the people, is founded in compact only, and instituted solely for the good of the whole." Section I, "Declaration of Rights," *Constitution of Maryland* (1776).

Something had changed however. The constitutional basis of authority was different. Power was delegated, stated in the written instrument, and no longer argued from the premises of an implied original contract found in custom, prescription, forensic history, political consensus, and the conventional practice of existing institutions. Different as the constitutional methods may seem—the old English constitution of prescriptive, customary rights and the written American constitutions—they were closer in legal theory to one another than they are to the twentieth-century British constitution in which authority is inherent in the sovereign.

Substance changed along with form, to be sure, but less than is sometimes thought. When Pennsylvania provided in its written constitution that people had a natural and unalienable right to worship according to individual conscience,[b] it codified a rule from its former colonial constitution, a rule not yet part of British constitutionalism. Moreover, the principle had not been involved in the revolutionary controversy. Although American whigs had been worried that London planned to institute an Anglican bishopric in the colonies and alarmed by talk that Roman Catholicism might become established in Quebec, Parliament had had no inclination to legislate religious practices. Liberty of conscience became a constitutional norm in the newly independent nation as a result of the Revolution and the new constitution making, not because of the Revolution. Surprisingly, the same was true for federalism. The concept of federalism had been so imperfectly perceived by both sides of the revolutionary controversy that it was not part of any plan for resolving the constitutional crisis[1]—except by implication when American whigs proposed separating the authority to regulate trade from the authority to legislate, vesting the authority to regulate in Parliament and the authority to legislate in colonial assemblies.

From one special perspective the framers of the state constitutions followed in the jurisprudential footsteps of the revolutionary whigs. Most of the principles that they drafted into constitutional clauses were adopted from the constitutional history of the mother country. Indeed, they incorporated substance not just from the current British constitution but from all of the earlier versions of the English constitution. From the oldest constitution, the ancient constitution, for example, the Virginia Constitution[2] kept the right to rebel,[c] the New Jersey Constitution retained the right of the

---

[b] "That all men have a natural and unalienable right to worship Almighty God according to the dictates of their own consciences and understanding: And that no man ought or of right can be compelled to attend any religious worship, or erect or support any place of worship, or maintain any ministry, contrary to, or against, his own free will and consent. . . ." Article II, "Declaration of the Rights of the Inhabitants," *Constitution of Pennsylvania* (1776).

[c] "[G]overnment is, or ought to be, instituted for the common benefit, protection, and

people to declare the original contract dissolved for cause,[d] and the New Hampshire Constitution extended the doctrine of consent by redefining it as the origin and foundation of government.[e] From a more familiar constitution—the seventeenth-century constitution which their ancestors had defended against Charles I and James II—the American framers adopted the power of impeachment (although no longer a criminal proceeding),[f] and the doctrine that bills of taxation originate in the popularly-elected house of the legislature.[g] From the "Glorious Revolution" constitution they took the rule that legislators are immune from arrest during term,[h] and the provisions prohibiting bills of attainder or *ex post facto* laws,[i] and prohibiting the executive from suspending statutes.[j] They also codified at least three of the rights constitutionally established as part of the Glorious Revolution settlement, the right to *habeas corpus*,[k] the right to bear arms,[l] and the right to a

---

security of the people . . . when any government shall be found inadequate or contrary to these purposes, a majority of the community hath an indubitable, unalienable, and indefeasible right to reform, alter, or abolish it, in such manner as shall be judged most conductive to the public weal." Section 3, "Bill of Rights," *Constitution of Virginia* (1776).

[d] "[W]hereas George the Third . . . has refused protection to the good people of these colonies, and, by assenting to sundry acts of the British parliament, attempted to subject them to the absolute dominion of that body; and has also made war upon them . . . —all civil authority under him is necessarily at an end, and a dissolution of government in each has consequently taken place." Preamble, *Constitution of New Jersey* (1776).

[e] "All men are born equally free and independent; therefore, all government of Right originates from the people, is founded in consent, and instituted for the general good." Article I, Section I, *Constitution of New Hampshire* (1784).

[f] Judgment was not to "extend further than to removal from office, and disqualification to hold or enjoy any place of honor, trust, or profit from this State." Article 33, *Constitution of New York* (1777).

[g] "All money-bills for the support of government shall originate in the house of assembly, and may be altered, amended, or rejected by the legislative council." Article 6, *Constitution of Delaware* (1776).

[h] "[N]o member of the house of representatives shall be arrested, or held to bail on mean process, during his going unto, returning from or his attending the general assembly." Chapter I, Section III, Article X, *Constitution of Massachusetts* (1780).

[i] "No Bill of Attainder or *ex post facto* Law shall be passed." Article I, Section 9, *Constitution of the United States* (1789).

[j] "That all powers of suspending laws, or the execution of laws, by any authority without consent of the Representatives of the people, is injurious to their rights, and ought not to be exercised." Section IV, "Declaration of Rights," *Constitution of North Carolina* (1776).

[k] "The Privilege of the Writ of Habeas Corpus shall not be suspended, unless when in Cases of Rebellion or Invasion the public Safety shall require it." Article I, Section 9, *Constitution of the United States* (1789).

[l] "[T]he people have a right to bear arms for the defence of themselves and the state." Section XIII, "Declaration of the Rights of the Inhabitants," *Constitution of Pennsylvania* (1776).

judiciary protected both by tenure at good behavior and by secured salaries.[m]

Of course, all inspiration was not old. Some of the principles and doctrines in the new written constitutions came right out of the American revolutionary controversy.[3] One was constitutional balance. If the constitutional crisis had taught colonial whigs any lesson it was that the fabled balanced British constitution had lost some vital weights. The power of monarchy or the "one" vested in the crown was supposed to check and balance the power of aristocracy or the "few" vested in the House of Lords and the power of democracy or the "many" vested in the House of Commons, and the two houses in turn balanced the crown and each other, so that no power in government could act arbitrarily and all power was "constitutional."[4] But the British constitution had not balanced for colonial whigs. All power emanated from the two houses of Parliament and the king, for all practical purposes, was of no consequence in the lawmaking process of the mother country. In their state and federal constitutions Americans recast the constitutional weights. Discarding the tripartite balance of monarchy, aristocracy, and democracy, they entrusted checks and balances to three branches of government—two known to the British constitution, the executive and legislative, and a third which they elevated to new importance, the judiciary.[n]

Drafters of the United States Constitution also drew on the revolutionary controversy. One lesson was from the disputes that had divided the colonies from Great Britain. They were a clue of what might cause friction between the states of the union and the new national government. We can see tailings of the Currency Act in the provision that, "No State shall . . . coin Money; emit Bills of Credit; make any Thing but gold or silver Coin a Tender in payment of Debts."[5] The framers were thinking in part of the debate over the authority of Parliament to bind the colonies in all cases whatsoever, when providing that "the laws of the United States . . . shall be the supreme Law of the Land; and the Judges in every State shall be bound thereby, any Thing in the Constitution or Laws of any State to the Contrary notwithstanding."[6] By saying that, "The Trial of all Crimes . . . shall be held in the State where the said Crimes shall have been committed,"[7] the Constitution

---

[m] "[F]or the security of the rights of the people, that the judges of the supreme judicial court should hold their offices so long as they behave well; . . . and that they should have honourable salaries, ascertained and established by standing laws." Article XXXV, "Bill of Rights," *Constitution of New Hampshire* (1784).

[n] "The legislative, executive, and judiciary departments shall be separate and distinct, so that neither exercise the powers properly belonging to the other." Article I, *Constitution of Georgia* (1777).

avoided replaying the controversies over laws such as the Act of 35 Henry VIII providing for trial in England either for defendants accused of treason or for imperial officials charged with a capital offense. And, in what was the most direct borrowing from the revolutionary controversy, the Commerce Clause of the United States Constitution codified the American whig doctrine of the imperial authority to regulate trade.º

Perhaps it cannot be attributed to the revolutionary controversy, but the fact is striking that American constitution drafters adopted from the old constitution of tripartite balances a major institution of prerogativism then virtually discarded by British constitutionalism. Colonial whigs and London "radicals" had wanted the veto to restore some balance to the constitution by making Parliament less supreme and less arbitrary. George III thought the authority to veto parliamentary legislation dormant. American framers revived it.P Although some of the early states constitutions made the legislative branch sovereign much like the British Parliament, by the turn of the century the constitutional norm was to give the executive a limited check over the will and pleasure of what the British called the democratic part of government. Indeed, if anything, American constitutionalists were consistent. The principle that they enshrined at the center of their state and federal constitutions, perhaps the principle that led them to write constitutions, was the same principle central to the revolutionary controversy: the rule of law.

The point has not yet been made, although it may be obvious by now, that a change had occurred in English legal thinking during the eighteenth century. As lawyers and parliamentarians in the mother country contemplated the meaning of sovereignty, they came to realize that rule of law, which had been so useful in the past as a constitutional restraint on the monarchy, did not restrain the legislature. Americans, adhering more stubbornly to the legacy of their shared English constitutional heritage and its inherent fear of arbitrary power, extended the concept of the rule of law from a restraint on the crown to being a restraint on the legislature, and, even more, a restraint on the sovereign.

The Massachusetts Constitution of 1780 gave the concept of the rule of law what in the eighteenth century would have been called its most "constitutional" expression. In the section on separation of powers, the Massa-

---

º "The Congress shall have Power to regulate Commerce with foreign Nations, and among the several States, and with the Indian Tribes." Article I, Section 8, *Constitution of the United States* (1789).

P "No bill or resolve of the senate or house of representatives shall become a law, and have force as such, until it shall have been laid before the governor for his revisal." Chapter I, Section I, Article II, *Constitution of Massachusetts* (1780).

chusetts document, America's seminal constitution, stipulated that the three
departments—executive, legislative, and judicial—should not exercise powers
properly belonging to another, "to the end that it may be a government of
laws and not of men."[8] Many people think that phrase the most famous
expression of the rule of law but that same constitution, the Massachusetts
Constitution of 1780, contained a second description of the rule of law that
is even more widely known: "[N]o subject shall be arrested, imprisoned,
despoiled, or deprived of his property, immunities, or privileges, put out of
the protection of the law, exiled, or deprived of life, liberty, or estate, but
by the judgment of his peers, or the law of the land."[9] Every eighteenth-
century lawyer recognized these words. They went back to the thirteenth
century and King John's pledge in Magna Carta to adhere to the rule of law.
"No free man shall be taken or imprisoned or disseised or outlawed or
exiled or in any way ruined, nor will we go or send against him, except by
the lawful judgement of his peers or by the law of the land."[10] The phraseology would be altered by the framers of the Fifth Amendment to the United
States Constitution. "Law of the land" became "due process of law"[q] but the
concept of rule by law remained consistent. American constitutionalism in
the nineteenth century would be the old English constitutionalism that was
being forgotten in the mother country, shifted from its old forum in Saint
Stephen's Chapel to the courts of law.

It may be misleading to say that the concept of the rule of law was
codified in the "due process" clause. It is more accurate to think of it as
codified in the very notion of a written constitution controlling sovereign
power, a point surely understood by Americans in the nineteenth century
when concocting their greatest departure from English and British constitutional law, the doctrine of judicial review. With the doctrine of judicial
review the concept of the rule of law realized its ultimate theoretical expression, and obtained what colonial whigs had found it lacked under the British
constitution of the late eighteenth century, an institutional guardian independent of legislative politics.

It will take answers to many questions not yet asked and a great deal of
research before anyone can say how much the American doctrine of judicial
review owed to colonial whig experience in the revolutionary crisis. The
most that now can be claimed is that the British process for determining
constitutional finality indicated to Americans the need for a dernier judge
that was neutral, nonpolitical, and not a party to any dispute. The British
constitutional process was summarized by Lord North in a speech to the
House of Commons. "Parliament themselves," he said, "are the only per-

[q] "No person shall . . . be deprived of life, liberty, or property, without due process of law."
Amendment V, *Constitution of the United States* (1789).

sons to judge of the propriety of their measures." That was not only the most fundamental rule in British constitutional law, it was the American constitutional predicament as a former colonial governor explained when reminding the Commons that for a person to be a judge in his own cause violated natural law. "Yet such is the precise situation in which we contend we ought to be placed, respecting the Americans, and for the denial of which we are ready to condemn our fellow-subjects to all the tortures enacted by the laws of treason."[11]

That was the constitutional predicament that colonial whigs had faced from the Stamp Act in 1765 to the coercive acts in 1774. The British constitution made Parliament the sole judge of its own authority. Although the fact may be incomprehensible to people of today, the solution favored by those American whigs who expressed their thoughts was to return to the old constitution, and to balance the sovereignty of Parliament with the prerogative of the king. George III would be the imperial arbiter of constitutional disputes between Parliament and the colonial assemblies. It was a whig solution both constitutionally revealing and historically surprising. It is revealing because it graphically demonstrates how committed colonial leaders were to the rule of constitutional law as they understood English constitutionalism, even if it meant making the crown an active, autonomous element in the tripartite balance of the imperial constitution. It is surprising because the course of subsequent history in the nineteenth century would lead us to expect that the Americans would have preferred the common-law courts as the dernier constitutional judge—the twelve judges of England, for example, or perhaps a combination of English, Scots, and Irish judges sitting *en banc*.[12] Following the Revolution, Americans had to remedy what they perceived as the fatal flaw in the British constitution: there was no final, neutral institution, independent of politics, with authority to hold the legislature to the rule of law. They would continue to separate the concept of the rule of law from legislative command and entrust its guardianship to a judiciary appointed for life and not removable by the political process. The British went the opposite way in the nineteenth century. They entrusted the rule of law to the will of the legislative majority.

ACKNOWLEDGMENTS
SHORT TITLES
NOTES
INDEX

ACKNOWLEDGMENTS

Leave from teaching responsibilities at New York University School of Law was provided by the Filomen D'Agostino Greenberg and Max E. Greenberg Faculty Research Fund at New York University School of Law, and by John Sexton, dean of New York University School of Law. As with the previous volumes in this Revolution-era series, the index was prepared by Carol B. Pearson of the Huntington Library. None of these books could have been completed without the splendid and professional assistance of the staff of the Library of the New York University School of Law, especially the remarkable Carol Alpert, the magnificent Elizabeth Evans, the dedicated Leslie Rich, and the unique Jay Shuman. Cite and substance checking was done by Barbara Wilcie Kern of East Ninth Street. The "Historiographical Preface" is in many respects the work of Richard B. Bernstein of New York Law School. It was his extensive, demanding, and scholarly criticism, joined to that of Thomas Mackey of the University of Louisville, that forced two revisions until there was a product that had their approval. A special debt of gratitude is owed to Gretchen Feltes, the Conservation Librarian of the New York University School of Law. It was she who discovered and brought to my attention the important fact that it was on a visit to New York University School of Law that Franklin Pierce told the students of the School of Law that during the Revolutionary War the slogan of the New Hampshire loyalists must have been, "Be Slaves and Die."

New York University School of Law

SHORT TITLES

Abingdon, *Thoughts on Burke's Letter*
> Willoughby Bertie, earl of Abingdon, *Thoughts on the Letter of Edmund Burke, Esq; to the Sheriffs of Bristol, on the Affairs of America.* 6th ed. Oxford, England [1777].

Acts of the Privy Council
> *Acts of the Privy Council of England. Colonial Series. Vol. IV. A.D. 1745–1766. Vol. V. A.D. 1766–1783.* Edited by James Munro. 1911, 1912.

Adams, *Writings*
> *The Writings of Samuel Adams.* Edited by Harry Alonzo Cushing. 4 vols. New York, 1904–08.

Addresses and Petitions of Common Council
> *Addresses, Remonstrances, and Petitions; Commencing the 24th of June, 1769, Presented to the King and Parliament, from the Court of Common Council, and the Livery in Common Hall assembled, with his Majesty's Answers: Likewise the Speech to the King, made by the late Mr. Alderman Beckford, When Lord Mayor of the City of London.* London, [1778].

Aldridge, "Paine and Dickinson"
> A. Owen Aldridge, "Paine and Dickinson," 11 *Early American Literature* (1976): 125–38.

American Archives
> *American Archives, Fourth Series. Containing a Documentary History of the English Colonies in North America From the King's Message to Parliament, of March 7, 1774, to the Declaration of Independence by the United States.* Vols. 1 and 2. Washington, D.C., 1837.

Anon., *Arguments to Prove*
> Anonymous, *Arguments to Prove the Interposition of the People to be Constitutional and Strictly Legal: In which the Necessity of a more Equal Representation of the People in Parliament is also Proved: and a Simple, Unobjectionable Mode of Equalizing the Representation is Suggested.* Dublin, 1783.

Anon., *Budget Inscribed*
> Anonymous, *The Budget. Inscribed to the Man, Who Thinks Himself Minister.* 9th Ed. London, 1764.

Anon., *Case of Great Britain*
> Anonymous, [Gervase Parker Bushe or George B. Butler,] *Case of Great Britain and America, Addressed to the King, and Both Houses of Parliament.* 3d ed. Boston, [1769].

Anon., *Celebrated Speech*
> Anonymous, *The Celebrated Speech of a Celebrated Commoner.* New ed. corrected. London, 1766.

Anon., *Common Sense Conferences*
> Anonymous, *Common Sense: in Nine Conferences, Between a British Merchant and a Candid Merchant of America, in their private capacities as friends; tracing the several causes of the present contests between the mother country and her American subjects; the fallacy of their prepossessions; and the ingratitude and danger of them; the reciprocal benefits of the national friendship; and the moral obligations of individuals which enforces it.* London, 1775.

Anon., *Conduct of Mansfield*
> Anonymous, *A Short Examination into the Conduct of Lord M[ans]f[iel]d, through the Affair of Mr. Wilkes.* London, 1768.

Anon., *Considerations Upon Rights of Colonists*
> Anonymous, *Considerations Upon the Rights of the Colonists to the Privileges of British Subjects, Introduc'd by a brief Review of the Rise and Progress of English Liberty, and concluded with some Remarks upon our present Alarming Situation.* New York, 1766.

Anon., *Constitutional Answer to Wesley*
> Anonymous, *A Constitutional Answer to the Rev. Mr. John Wesley's Calm Address to the American Colonies.* London, 1775.

Anon., *Examination of the Legality*
> Anonymous, *A Candid Examination of the Legality of the Warrant Issued by the Secretaries of State For Apprehending the Printers, Publishers, &c. of a late Interesting Paper.* London, 1764.

Anon., *Fair Trial*
> Anonymous, *A Fair Trial of the Important Question, or the Rights of Election Asserted; Against the Doctrine of Incapacity by Expulsion, or by Resolution: Upon True Constitutional Principles, the Real Law of Parliament, the Common Right of the Subject, and the Determinations of the House of Commons.* London, 1769.

Anon., *Four Letters*
> Anonymous, *Four Letters on Interesting Subjects.* Philadelphia, 1776.

Anon., *Letter to Rev. Cooper*
> Anonymous, *A Letter to the Rev. Dr. Cooper, on the Origin of Civil Government; in Answer to his Sermon, Preached before the Univeristy of Oxford, on the Day appointed by Proclamation for a General Fast.* London, 1777.

Anon., *Licentiousness Unmask'd*
> Anonymous, *Licentiousness Unmask'd; or Liberty Explained.* London, n. d.

Anon., *Observations Upon the Authority*
> Anonymous, *Observations Upon the Authority, Manner and Circumstances of the Apprehension and Confinement of Mr. Wilkes. Addressed to Free-Born Englishmen.* London, 1763.

Anon., *Policy of the Laws*
> Anonymous, *An Inquiry into the Policy of the Laws, Affecting the Popish Inhabitants of Ireland, Preceded by a Short Political Analysis of the History and Constitution of Ireland, In which the Rights of Colonists and Planters are briefly mentioned . . . with some Hints respecting America.* Dublin, 1775.

Anon., *Prospect of Consequences*
> Anonymous, *A Prospect of the Consequences of the Present Conduct of Great Britain Towards America.* London, 1776.

Anon., *Serious and Impartial Observations*
> Anonymous, *Serious and Impartial Observations on the Blessings of Liberty and Peace. Addressed to Persons of all Parties. Inviting them also to enter into that Grand ASSOCIATION, which is able to secure the Safety and Happiness of the British Empire.* London, 1776.

Anon., *Some Reasons for Approving Gloucester's Plan*
> Anonymous, *Some Reasons for Approving of the Dean of Gloucester's Plan, of Separating from the Colonies; with a Proposal for a Further Improvement.* London, 1775.

Anon., *Supremacy of Legislature*
> Anonymous, *The Supremacy of the British Legislature over the Colonies, Candidly Discussed.* London, 1775.

Anon., *To Tax Themselves*
> Anonymous, *An Argument in Defence of the Exclusive Right Claimed by the Colonies to Tax Themselves; With A Review of the Laws of England, Relative to Representation and Taxation. To which is Added, an Account of the*

Rise of the Colonies, and the Manner in which the Rights of the Subjects within the realm were communicated to those that went to America, with the Exercise of those Rights from the First Settlement to the Present Time. London, 1774.

Anon., *To the People of Britain in General*
Anonymous, *An Address to the People of Great-Britain in General, the Members of Parliament, and the Leading Gentlemen of Opposition in Particular, on the Present Crisis of American Politics.* Bristol, 1776.

"Another Origin of Judicial Review"
John Phillip Reid, "Another Origin of Judicial Review: The Constitutional Crisis of 1776 and the Need for a Dernier Judge," *New York University Law Review* 64 (1989): 963–89.

Appleby, "Different Independence"
Joyce Appleby, "A Different Kind of Independence: The Postwar Restructing of the Historical Study of Early America," *William and Mary Quarterly* 50 (1993): 245–67.

Authority of Law
John Phillip Reid, *Constitutional History of the American Revolution: The Authority of Law.* Madison, Wisc., 1993.

Authority of Rights
John Phillip Reid, *Constitutional History of the American Revolution: The Authority of Rights.* Madison, Wisc., 1986.

Authority to Legislate
John Phillip Reid, *Constitutional History of the American Revolution: The Authority to Legislate.* Madison, Wisc., 1991.

Authority to Tax
John Phillip Reid, *Constitutional History of the American Revolution: The Authority to Tax.* Madison, Wisc., 1987.

Bailyn, *Ideological Origins*
Bernard Bailyn, *The Ideological Origins of the American Revolution.* Cambridge, Mass., 1967.

Bailyn, *Pamphlets*
Pamphlets of the American Revolution, 1750–1776. Vol. 1. Edited by Bernard Bailyn. Cambridge, Mass., 1965.

Bailyn, "Revolution and Enlightenment"
Bernard Bailyn, "The Revolution and Enlightenment Ideas: A Critique," in *The American Revolution—How Revolutionary Was It?* Edited by George Athan Billias. New York, 1965, pp. 87–100.

Baldwin, *New England Clergy*
Alice M. Baldwin, *The New England Clergy and The American Revolution.* New York, 1958.

Bancroft, *History*
>   George Bancroft, *History of the United States of America From the Discovery of the Continent*. Vol. 3. Boston, 1878.

[Bancroft,] *Remarks*
>   [Edward Bancroft,] *Remarks on the Review of the Controversy Between Great Britain and her Colonies. In which the Errors of its Author are exposed, and the Claims of the Colonies vindicated, Upon the Evidence of Historical Facts and authentic Records.* London, 1769.

Becker, *History of Political Parties*
>   Carl Becker, *History of Political Parties in the Province of New York, 1763–1776.* Madison, Wisc., 1909.

Billias, "Introduction"
>   George Athan Billias, "Introduction," in *The American Revolution—How Revolutionary Was It?* Edited by George Athan Billias. New York, 1965, pp. 1–8.

Blackstone, *Commentaries*
>   William Blackstone, *Commentaries on the Laws of England.* 4 vols. Oxford, England, 1765–1769.

Bloch, "Constitution and Culture"
>   Ruth H. Bloch, "The Constitution and Culture," *William and Mary Quarterly* 44 (1987): 550–55.

Boston Chronicle
>   *The Boston Chronicle.* (Weekly newspaper).

Boston Evening-Post
>   *The Boston Evening-Post.* (Weekly newspaper).

Boston Gazette
>   *The Boston Gazette and Country Journal.* (Weekly newspaper).

Boston News-Letter
>   *The Massachusetts Gazette and Boston News-Letter,* also sometimes *The Massachusetts Gazette and the Boston News-Letter,* or *The Boston News-Letter.* (Weekly newspaper).

Briefs of Revolution
>   *The Briefs of the American Revolution: Constitutional Arguments Between Thomas Hutchinson, Governor of Massachusetts Bay, and James Bowdoin for the Council and John Adams for the House of Representatives.* Edited by John Phillip Reid. New York, 1981.

Brown, "Democracy"
>   Robert E. Brown, "Democracy in Colonial Massachusetts," *New England Quarterly* 25 (1952): 291–313.

Brown, "Economic Democracy"
>   Robert E. Brown, "Economic Democracy Before the Constitution," *American Quarterly* 7 (1955): 257–74.

Brown, *Revolutionary Politics*
Richard D. Brown, *Revolutionary Politics in Massachusetts: The Boston Committee of Correspondence and the Towns, 1772–1774.* New York, 1976.

Brown, "Revolution as Conservative Movement"
Robert E. Brown, "The Revolution as a Conservative Movement in Massachusetts," in *The American Revolution—How Revolutionary Was It?* Edited by George Athan Billias. New York, 1965, pp. 71–77.

Burgh, *Political Disquisitions*
J. Burgh, *Political Disquisitions; or, An Enquiry into public Errors, Defects, and Abuses. Illustrated by, and established upon Facts and Remarks, extracted from a Variety of Authors, Ancient and Modern.* 3 vols. Philadelphia, 1775.

Burke Writings
The Writings and Speeches of Edmund Burke. Volume II Party, Parliament, and the American Crisis. Edited by Paul Langford. Oxford, England, 1981.

[Burnet,] *Submission to Supream Authority*
[Gilbert Burnet,] *An Enquiry Into the Measures of Submission to the Supream Authority: And of the Grounds upon which it may be lawful or necessary for Subjects, to defend their Religion, Lives, and Liberties.* n.i., [1688].

[Butler,] *Standing Army*
[John Butler,] *A Consultation On the Subject of a Standing Army, Held at the King's-Arms Tavern, On the Twenty-eighth Day of February 1763.* London, 1763.

Care, *English Liberties Boston Edition*
Henry Care, *English Liberties, or the Free-Born's Subject's Inheritance; Containing Magna Charta, Charta de Foresta, The Statute De Tallagio non concedendo, The Habeas Corpus Act, and several other Statutes; with Comments on each of them.* 5th ed. Boston, 1721.

Cato's Letters
Cato's Letters: or, Essays on Liberty, Civil and Religious, And other Important Subjects. In Four Volumes. 6th ed. London, 1755.

Chauncy, *Civil Magistrates*
Charles Chauncy, *Civil Magistrates must be just, ruling in The Fear of God. A Sermon Preached before His Excellency William Shirley, Esq; The Honourable His Majesty's Council, and House of Representatives, of the Province of the Massachusetts-Bay in N. England; May 27, 1747. Being The Anniversary for The Election of His Majesty's Council for Said Province.* Boston, 1747.

Cohen, "Revolution and Natural Law"
Lester H. Cohen, "The American Revolution and Natural Law Theory," *Journal of the History of Ideas* 39 (1978): 491–502.

Colbourn, *Lamp of Experience*
H. Trevor Colbourn, *The Lamp of Experience: Whig History and the Intellectual Origins of the American Revolution.* Chapel Hill, N.C., 1965.

Collection of Irish Letters
> *A Collection of The Letters which have been addressed to the Volunteers of Ireland, on the subject of a Parliamentary Reform.* London, 1783.

Commemoration Ceremony
> *Commemoration Ceremony in Honor of the Two Hundredth Anniversary of the First Continental Congress in the United States House of Representatives.* House Document No. 93–413, 93d Congress, 2d Session. Washington, D.C., 1975.

Commons Debates 1621
> *Commons Debates 1621.* Edited by Wallace Notestein, Francis Helen Relf, and Hartley Simpson. 7 vols. New Haven, Conn., 1935.

Commons Debates 1628
> *Commons Debates 1628.* Edited by Robert C. Johnson, Mary Frear Keeler, Maija Cole, and William B. Bidwell. 6 vols. New Haven, Conn., 1977–1983.

Concept of Liberty
> John Phillip Reid, *The Concept of Liberty in the Age of the American Revolution.* Chicago, 1988.

Concept of Representation
> John Phillip Reid, *The Concept of Representation in the Age of the American Revolution.* Chicago, 1989.

Conference of Both Houses
> *A Conference Desired by the Lords and had by a Committee of both Houses, Concerning the Rights and Privileges of the Subjects. Discoursed by Sir Dudley Digges. Sir Edward Littleton Knight, now Lord Keeper. Master Selden. Sir Edward Cooke. With the Objections by Sir Robert Heath Knight then Attorney Generall, and the Answers. 3 Apr. 4 Car. 1628.* London, 1642.

Conway, *Peace Speech*
> Henry Seymour Conway, *The Speech of General Conway, Member of Parliament for Saint Edmondsbury, on moving in the House of Commons, (On the 5th of May, 1780).* London, 1781.

Cornell, "Early American History"
> Saul Cornell, "Early American History in a Postmodern Age," *William and Mary Quarterly* 50 (1993): 329–41.

Critical Review
> *The Critical Review: Or Annals of Literature by a Society of Gentlemen.* (Monthly magazine, London).

Davis, *Reports*
> Sir John Davis [Davies], *Les Reports Des Cases & Matters en Ley, Resolves & Adjudges en les Courts del Roy en Ireland.* London, 1674.

"Declaratory Debates"
> "Debates on the Declaratory Act and the Repeal of the Stamp Act, 1766," *American Historical Review* 17 (1912): 563–86.

Degler, "Preface 3"
    Carl N. Degler, "Preface 3," in *Pivotal Interpretations of American History*.
    Edited by Carl N. Degler. Vol. 1. New York, 1966.

Delaware House Minutes (1765–1770)
    Votes and Proceedings of the House of Representatives of the Government of
    the Counties of New Castle, Kent and Sussex, upon Delaware. At Sessions held
    at New Castle in the Years 1765–1766–1767–1768–1769–1770. Dover, Del.,
    1931.

Demophilus, *Genuine Principles*
    Demophilus, *The Genuine Principles of the Ancient Saxon, or English Consti-*
    tution Carefully collected from the best Authorities; With some Observations,
    on their peculiar fitness, for the United Colonies in general, and Pennsylvania
    in particular. Philadelphia, 1776.

Dickinson, *Letters*
    John Dickinson, *Letters from a Farmer in Pennsylvania to the Inhabitants of*
    the British Colonies (1768), reprinted in Dickinson, *Writings*, at 305–406.

Dickinson, *Writings*
    The Writings of John Dickinson: Political Writings 1764–1774. Edited by Paul
    Leicester Ford. Philadelphia, 1895.

Fisher, *True History*
    Sydney George Fisher, *The True History of the American Revolution*. Phila-
    delphia, 1912.

Fiske, *Importance of Righteousness*
    Nathan Fiske, *The Importance of Righteousness to the Happiness, and the*
    Tendency of Oppression to the Misery of a People; illustrated in two Dis-
    courses Delivered at Brookfield, July 4. 1774. Boston, 1774.

[Fitch et al.,] *Reasons Why*
    [Thomas Fitch, Jared Ingersoll, Ebenezer Silliman, and George Wyllys,] *Rea-*
    sons Why the British Colonies, in America, Should not be Charged with
    Internal Taxes, by Authority of Parliament; Humbly offered, For Considera-
    tion, In Behalf of the Colony of Connecticut. New Haven, Conn., 1764.

[Forster,] *Answer to the Question Stated*
    [Nathaniel Forster,] *An Answer to a Pamphlet Entitled, "The Question Stated,*
    Whether the Freeholders of Middlesex forfeited their Right by Voting for Mr.
    Wilkes at the last Election? In a Letter from a Member of Parliament to one of
    his Constituents." London, 1769.

Fox, *Speech of 2 July*
    Charles James Fox, *The Speech of the Right Honourable Charles James Fox,*
    on American Independence: Spoken in the House of Commons, On Tuesday,
    July 2, 1782. London, [1782].

Gazette & News-Letter
    The Massachusetts Gazette and Boston News-Letter.

Gazette & Post-Boy
> *The Massachusetts Gazette and Boston Post-Boy and the Advertiser.*

Gentleman's Magazine
> *The Gentleman's Magazine and Historical Chronicle* (Monthly magazine, London).

Georgia Commons House Journal
> *The Colonial Records of the State of Georgia. Volume XIV. Journal of the Commons House of Assembly January 17, 1763, to December 24, 1768, Inclusive. Volume XV. Journal of the Commons House of Assembly October 30, 1769, to June 16, 1782, Inclusive.* Atlanta, Ga., 1907.

[Goodricke,] *Observations on Price's Theory*
> [Henry Goodricke,] *Observations on Dr. Price's Theory and Principles of Civil Liberty and Government, Preceded by a Letter to a Friend, on the Pretensions of the American Colonies, in respect of Right and Equity.* York, England, 1776.

Gordon, *Discourse Preached*
> William Gordon, *A Discourse Preached December 15th 1774. Being the Day Recommended by the Provincial Congress; And Afterwards at the Boston Lecture.* London, 1775.

Greene, "Changing Interpretations"
> Jack P. Greene, "Changing Interpretations of Early American Politics," in *The Reinterpretation of Early American History.* Edited by Ray Allen Billington. San Marino, Calif., 1966, pp. 151–84.

Greene, "Origins"
> Jack P. Greene, "Origins of the American Revolution: A Constitutional Interpretation," in *The Framing and Ratification of the Constitution.* Edited by Leonard W. Levy and Dennis J. Mahoney. New York, 1987, pp. 36–53.

Greene, *Peripheries and Center*
> Jack P. Greene, *Peripheries and Center: Constitutional Development in the Extended Polities of the British Empire and the United States, 1607–1788.* Athens, Ga., 1986.

Grenville Letterbooks
> Letterbooks of George Grenville. ST 7, Huntington Library, San Marino, Calif.

Grenville Papers
> *The Grenville Papers: Being the Correspondence of Richard Grenville Earl Temple, K. G., and The Right Hon. George Grenville, their Friends and Contemporaries.* 4 vols. Edited by William James Smith. London, 1852–1853.

Hale, "Reflections"
> Matthew Hale, "Reflections by the Lrd. Chiefe Justice Hale on Mr. Hobbes His Dialogue of the Lawe," printed in W. S. Holdsworth, *A History of English Law.* London 5 (1924): 500–13.

Hamilton, *Farmer Refuted*
> Alexander Hamilton, *The Farmer Refuted: or A more impartial and comprehensive View of the Dispute between Great-Britain and the Colonies, Intended as a Further Vindication of the Congress* (1775), reprinted in *The Papers of Alexander Hamilton. Vol. 1.* Edited by Harold C. Syrett. New York, 1961, pp. 81–165.

Handlin, *Popular Sources*
> *The Popular Sources of Political Authority: Documents on the Massachusetts Constitution of 1780.* Edited by Oscar and Mary Handlin. Cambridge, Mass., 1966.

[Hartley,] *Appeal to Juries*
> [David Hartley,] *The Right of Appeal to Juries in Causes of Excise, Asserted.* London, [1763].

Hartley, *Speech and Motions*
> David Hartley, *Speech and Motions Made in the House of Commons, on Monday, the 27th of March, 1775. Together with a Draught of a Letter of Requisition to the Colonies.* [2d ed. London, 1775].

Hawles, *Englishman's Right*
> Sir John Hawles, *The Englishman's Right: A Dialogue Between a Barrister at Law, and a Juryman.* Dublin, 1732.

[Heath,] *Case of Devon Excise*
> [B. Heath,] *The Case of the County of Devon, With Respect to the Consequences of the New Excise Duty on Cyder and Perry. Published by the Direction of the Committee appointed at the General Meeting of that County to superintend the Application for the Repeal of that Duty.* London, 1763.

Hoadly, *Works*
> *The Works of Benjamin Hoadly, D.D. Successively Bishop of Bangor, Hereford, Salisbury, and Winchester.* 3 vols. London, 1773.

Hopkins, *Rights*
> Stephen Hopkins, *The Rights of Colonies Examined* (1765), reprinted in Bailyn, *Pamphlets*, pp. 507–22.

Howard, *Road from Runnymede*
> A. E. Dick Howard, *The Road from Runnymede: Magna Carta and Constitutionalism in America.* Charlottesville, Va., 1968.

"In Accordance with Usage"
> John Phillip Reid, "In Accordance with Usage: The Authority of Custom, the Stamp Act Debate, and the Coming of the American Revolution," *Fordham Law Review* 45 (1976): 335–68.

"In a Defensive Rage"
> John Phillip Reid, "In a Defensive Rage: The Uses of the Mob, the Justification in Law, and the Coming of the American Revolution," *New York University Law Review* 49 (1974): 1043–91.

In a Defiant Stance
John Phillip Reid, *In a Defiant Stance: The Conditions of Law in Massachusetts Bay, the Irish Comparison, and the Coming of the American Revolution.* University Park, Pa., 1977.

In a Rebellious Spirit
John Phillip Reid, *In a Rebellious Spirit: The Argument of Facts, the Liberty Riot, and the Coming of the American Revolution.* University Park, Pa., 1979.

In Defiance of the Law
John Phillip Reid, *In Defiance of the Law: The Standing- Army Controversy, the Two Constitutions, and the Coming of the American Revolution.* Chapel Hill, N.C., 1981.

"In Our Contracted Sphere"
John Phillip Reid, "'In Our Contracted Sphere': The Constitutional Contract, the Stamp Act Crisis, and the Coming of the American Revolution," *Columbia Law Review* 76 (1976): 21–47.

"In the Taught Tradition"
John Phillip Reid, "In the Taught Tradition: The Meaning of Law in Massachusetts-Bay Two Hundred Years Ago," *Suffolk University Law Review* 14 (1980): 931–74.

"Irrelevance of the Declaration"
John Phillip Reid, "The Irrelevance of the Declaration," in *Law in the American Revolution and the Revolution in the Law.* Edited by Hendrik Hartog. New York, 1981, pp. 46–89.

Jenkins, *Works*
David Jenkins, *The Works of the Eminent and Learned Judge Jenkins Upon Divers Statutes Concerning the King's Prerogative and the Liberty of the Subject: Now Reprinted from the Original Authentick Copy, Written and Published by Himself, when Prisoner in Newgate.* London, 1681.

Jenkins, *Works of Judge Jenkins*
David Jenkins, *The Works of that Grave and Learned Lawyer Judge Jenkins, Prisoner in Newgate. Upon Divers Statutes, Concerning, the Liberty, and Freedome of the Subject. With a perfect Table thereto annexed.* London, 1648.

Johnson, *Notes on Pastoral*
Samuel Johnson, *Notes Upon the Phoenix Edition of the Pastoral Letter. Part I.* London, 1694.

[Johnson,] *Some Important Observations*
[Stephen Johnson,] *Some Important Observations, Occasioned by, and adapted to, the Publick Fast, Ordered by Authority, December 18th, A.D. 1765.* Newport, R.I., 1766.

[Jones,] *Constitutional Criterion*
[William Jones,] *The Constitutional Criterion: By a Member of the University of Cambridge.* London, 1768.

Journal of Burgesses
   Journals of the House of Burgesses of Virginia [Vol. 10] 1761–1765, [Vol. 11]
   1766–1769, [Vol. 12] 1770–1772, [Vol. 13] 1773–1776 Including the records of
   the Committee of Correspondence. Edited by John Pendleton Kennedy. Rich-
   mond, Va., 1905, 1906, 1907.

Journal of New York Assembly (1766–1776)
   Journal of the Votes and Proceedings of the General Assembly of the Colony of
   New-York, From 1766 to 1776 Inclusive. Reprinted in pursuance of a joint
   resolution of the Legislature of the State of New-York, passed 30 April, 1820.
   Albany, N.Y., 1820.

Journal of the First Congress
   Journal of the Proceedings of the Congress, Held at Philadelphia, September 5,
   1774. Philadelphia, 1774.

Journal of the Times
   Boston Under Military Rule 1768–1769 as Revealed in a Journal of the Times.
   Compiled by Oliver Morton Dickerson. Boston, 1936.

Journals of Congress
   Journals of the Continental Congress 1774–1789. Edited by Worthington
   Chauncey Ford, et al. 34 vols. Washington, D.C., 1904–1937.

"Junius," *Junius*
   ["Junius,"] *Junius.* 2 vols. London, [1772].

"Jurisprudence of Liberty"
   John Phillip Reid, "The Jurisprudence of Liberty: The Ancient Constitution in
   the Legal Historiography of the Seventeenth and Eighteenth Centuries," in
   The Roots of Liberty: Magna Carta, Ancient Constitution, and the Anglo-
   American Tradition of Rule of Law. Edited by Ellis Sandoz. Columbia, Mo.,
   1993, pp. 147–231.

Keir, *Constitutional History*
   Sir David Lindsay Keir, *The Constitutional History of Modern Britain Since*
   1845. 8th ed. Princeton, N.J., 1966.

Kemp, "Parliamentary Sovereignty"
   Betty Kemp, "Parliamentary Sovereignty," *London Review of Books*, 5 no. 4
   (18 January 1984): pp. 12–14.

Kerber, "Revolutionary Generation"
   Linda Kerber, "The Revolutionary Generation: Ideology, Politics, and Culture
   in the Early Republic," in *The New American History*. Edited by Eric Foner.
   Philadephia, 1990, pp. 25–49.

Knollenberg, "Adams and the Tea Party"
   Bernhard Knollenberg, "Did Samuel Adams provoke the Boston Tea Party
   and the Clash at Lexington?" *Proceedings of the American Antiquarian Soci-*
   ety 70 (1960): 494–503.

"L.," *Letter to G[renville]*
  "L.," *A Letter to G. G. Stiff in Opinions, always in the wrong.* London, 1767.

Lee, *Appeal to Justice*
  [Arthur] Lee, *An Appeal to the Justice and Interests of the People of Great Britain, in the Present Dispute with America.* 4th ed. London, 1774.

Lee, *Election Sermon*
  Jonathan Lee, *A Sermon Delivered before the General Assembly of the Colony of Connecticut, at Hartford; On the Day of the Anniversary Election, May 8th, 1766.* New London, Conn., 1766.

Lee Letters
  The Letters of Richard Henry Lee, 1762–1778. Edited by James Curtis Ballagh. 2 vols., New York, 1911–1914.

Letters of Delegates to Congress
  Letters of Delegates to Congress: 1774–1789. 12 vols. Edited by Paul H. Smith. Washington, D.C., 1976–1985.

[Lind,] *Thirteenth Parliament*
  [John Lind,] *Remarks on the Principal Acts of the Thirteenth Parliament of Great Britain. Vol. I. Containing Remarks on the Acts relating to the Colonies. With a Plan of Reconciliation.* London, 1775.

Lockwood, *Connecticut Election Sermon*
  Samuel Lockwood, *Civil Rulers an Ordinance of God, for Good to Mankind. A Sermon, Preached Before the General Assembly, of the Colony of Connecticut, at Hartford; On the Day of their Anniversary Election, May 12th, 1774.* New London, Conn., 1774.

London Magazine
  The London Magazine or Gentleman's Monthly Intelligencer. (Monthly magazine, London).

Lucas, *Divelina Libera*
  Charles Lucas, *Divelina Libera: An Apology for the Civil Rights and Liberties of the Commons and Citizens of Dublin.* Dublin, 1744.

Madden, "Origins"
  Frederick Madden, "Some Origins and Purposes in the Formation of British Colonial Government," in *Essays in Imperial Government Presented to Margery Perham.* Edited by Kenneth Robinson and Frederick Madden. Oxford, England, 1963.

Madden, "Relevance of Experience"
  A. F. McC. Madden, "1066, 1776 and All That: The Relevance of English Medieval Experience of 'Empire' to Later Imperial Constitutional Issues," in *Perspectives of Empire: Essays Presented to Gerald S. Graham.* Edited by John E. Flint and Glyndwr Williams. New York, 1973.

Main, *Social Structure*
Jackson Turner Main, *The Social Structure of Revolutionary America*. Princeton, N.J., 1965.

Marvell, *Account*
Andrew Marvell, *An Account of the Growth of Popery and Arbitrary Government in England*. Amsterdam, 1677.

Mayhew, *Snare Broken*
Jonathan Mayhew, *The Snare broken. A Thanksgiving-Discourse, Preached At the Desire of the West Church in Boston, N.E. Friday May 23, 1766, Occasioned by the Repeal of the Stamp-Act*. Boston, 1766.

McAdam, *Johnson and Law*
E. L. McAdam, *Dr. Johnson and the English Law*. Syracuse, N.Y., 1951.

McIlwain, *Revolution*
Charles Howard McIlwain, *The American Revolution: A Constitutional Interpretation*. Ithaca, N.Y., 1958.

[Mitchell,] *Present State*
[John Mitchell,] *The Present State of Great Britain and North America, with Regard to Agriculture, Population, Trade and Manufactures, impartially considered*. London, 1767.

Morgan, "American Revolution"
Edmund S. Morgan, "The American Revolution: Revisions in Need of Revising," in *In Search of Early America: The William and Mary Quarterly, 1943–1993*. Williamsburgh, Va., 1993, pp. 44–53.

Morgan, *Birth*
Edmund S. Morgan, *The Birth of the Republic, 1763–89*. Chicago, 1956.

Morgan, *Challenge*
Edmund S. Morgan, *The Challenge of the American Revolution*. New York, 1976.

Morgan, "Colonial Ideas"
Edmund S. Morgan, "Colonial Ideas of Parliamentary Power 1764–1766," *William and Mary Quarterly* 5 (1948): 311–41.

Morgan, *Prologue*
Prologue to Revolution: Sources and Documents on the Stamp Act Crisis, 1764–1766. Edited by Edmund S. Morgan. Chapel Hill, N.C., 1959.

[Mulgrave,] *Letter from a Member*
[Mulgrave, C. J. Phipps, Lord,] *A Letter from a Member of Parliament to One of his Constituents, on the Late Proceedings of the House of Commons in the Middlesex Elections*. London, 1769.

New Jersey Votes and Proceedings (1769)
Votes and Proceedings of the General Assembly of the Province of New-Jersey.

At a Session of General Assembly, began at Burlington, October 10, 1769, and continued till the 6th Day of December following. Woodbridge, N.J., 1769.

New York Colonial Documents
Documents Relative to the Colonial History of the State of New-York; Procured in Holland, England, and France. Edited by E. B. O'Callaghan. Vol. 7. Albany, N.Y., 1856.

[Nicholas,] *Proceedings of 1620–21*
[Edward Nicholas,] *Proceedings and Debates of the House of Commons, in 1620 and 1621.* 2 vols. Oxford, England, 1766.

North Carolina Colonial Records
The Colonial Records of North Carolina, Published Under the Supervision of the Trustees of the Public Libraries, By Order of the General Assembly. Vols. 7, 8, 9, and 10. Edited by William L. Saunders, Raleigh, N.C., 1888, 1890.

Paley, *Principles of Philosophy*
William Paley, *The Principles of Moral and Political Philosophy.* London, 1785.

Parliamentary History
The Parliamentary History of England, From the Earliest Period to the Year 1803. 36 vols. London, 1806–1820.

Pemberton, *Lord North*
W. Baring Pemberton, *Lord North.* London, 1938.

Pennsylvania Archives
Pennsylvania Archives: Eighth Series [Votes and Proceedings of the House of Representatives.] 8 vols. [Harrisburg, Pa.,] 1931–1935.

Petyt, *Lex Parliamentaria*
G[eorge] P[etyt], *Lex Parliamentaria: or, a Treatise of the Law and Custom of the Parliaments of England.* London, 1690.

Pocock, *Politics*
J. G. A. Pocock, *Politics, Language and Time: Essays on Political Thought and History.* New York, 1971.

Political Register
The Political Register; and Impartial Review of New Books. (Monthly magazine, London).

Price, *Two Tracts*
Richard Price, *Two Tracts on Civil Liberty, the War with America, and the Debts and Finances of the Kingdom: with a General Introduction and Supplement.* London, 1778.

Price, *Two Tracts: Tract One*
Richard Price, *Observations on the Nature of Civil Liberty, the Principles of Government, and the Justice and Policy of the War with America.* 8th Edition. London, 1778, reprinted in Price, *Two Tracts,* pp. 1–112.

Prior Documents
> *A Collection of Interesting, Authentic Papers, Relative to the Dispute Between Great Britain and America; Shewing the Causes and Progress of that Misunderstanding, From 1764 to 1775.* London, 1777.

Proceedings and Debates
> *Proceedings and Debates of the British Parliaments Respecting North America 1754–1783.* Edited by R. C. Simmons and P. D. G. Thomas. 6 vols. White Plains, N.Y., 1982–1987.

Proceedings and Debates of Parliaments
> *Proceedings and Debates of the British Parliaments respecting North America.* Edited by Leo Francis Stock. 5 vols. Washington, D.C., 1924–1941.

Proceedings Against Manwaring
> *The Proceedings of the Lords and Commons In the Year 1628. Against Roger Manwaring Doctor in Divinty, [The Sacheverell of those Days] For Two Seditious High-flying Sermons, intitled, Religion and Allegiance.* London, 1709.

Protests of Lords of Ireland
> *A Collection of the Protests of the Lords of Ireland, From 1634 to 1771.* Dublin, 1772.

Rakove, *Beginnings*
> Jack N. Rakove, *The Beginnings of National Politics: An Interpretative History of the Continental Congress.* Baltimore, 1979.

[Ramsay,] *Historical Essay*
> [Allan Ramsay,] *An Historical Essay on the English Constitution: Or, An impartial Inquiry into the Elective Power of the People, from the first Establishment of the Saxons in this Kingdom. Wherein the Right of Parliament, to Tax our distant Provinces, is explained, and justified, upon such constitutional Principles as will afford an equal Security to the Colonists, as to their Brethren at Home.* London, 1771.

[Rawson,] *Revolution in New England*
> [Edward Rawson,] *The Revolution in New England Justified, And the People there Vindicated From the Aspersions cast upon them by Mr. John Palmer, In his Pretended Answer to the Declaration, Published by the Inhabitants of Boston, and the Country adjacent, on the day when they secured their late Oppressors, who acted by an Illegal and Arbitrary Commission from the Late King James.* Boston, 1691.

Remonstrance of the Cities (1659)
> *A Remonstrance and Protestation of the Well-affected People in the Cities of London, Westminster, and the other Cities, Counties and Places within the Commonwealth of England, against those Officers of the Army, who put force upon, and interrupted the Parliament, the 13th Octob. 1659, and against all pretended Powers or Authoritys that they have or shall set up, to Rule or Govern this Common-Wealth That is not Established by Parliament.* London, 1659.

Revolution Documents
>   *Documents of the American Revolution 1770–1783.* Edited by K. G. Davies. Vols. 1 to 16. Dublin, 1972–1981.

Revolutionary Virginia
>   *Revolutionary Virginia The Road to Independence—Volume I: Forming Thunderclouds and the First Convention, 1763–1774. A Documentary Record.* Compiled by William J. Van Schreeven, edited by Robert L. Scribner. *Volume II: The Committees and the Second Convention, 1773–1775. A Documentary Record.* Compiled by William J. Van Schreeven and Robert L. Scribner. *Volume III: The Breaking Storm and the Third Convention, 1775. A Documentary Record.* Compiled and edited by Robert L. Scribner and Brent Tarter. *Volume IV: The Committee of Safety and the Balance of Forces, 1775. A Documentary Record.* Compiled and edited by Robert L. Scribner and Brent Tarter. *Volume V: The Clash of Arms and the Fourth Convention, 1775–1776. A Documentary Record.* Compiled and edited by Robert L. Scribner and Brent Tarter. *Volume VI: The Time for Decision, 1776. A Documentary Record.* Compiled and edited by Robert L. Scribner and Brent Tarter. [Charlottesville, Va.,] 1973–1979.

Rhode Island Colony Records
>   *Records of the Colony of Rhode Island and Providence Plantations in New England.* Edited by John Russell Bartlett. 10 vols. Providence, R.I., 1856–1865.

Rossiter, "Shaping American Tradition"
>   Clinton Rossiter, "The Shaping of the American Tradition," *William and Mary Quarterly* 11 (1954): 519–35.

"Rule of Law"
>   John Phillip Reid, "The Rule of Law," in *The Blackwell Encyclopedia of the American Revolution.* Edited by Jack P. Greene and J. R. Pole. Oxford, England, 1991, pp. 629–33.

Ryder, "Parliamentary Diaries"
>   "Parliamentary Diaries of Nathaniel Ryder, 1764–7," edited by P. D. G. Thomas. *Camden Miscellany Vol. XXIII.* Camden Society, 4th Series, vol. 7. London, [1969], pp. 229–351.

St. Patrick's Anti-Stamp Chronicle
>   *St. Patrick's Anti-Stamp Chronicle: Or, Independent Magazine, of News, Politics, and Literary Entertainment.* Dublin.

Schlesinger, "American Revolution"
>   Arthur Meier Schlesinger, "The American Revolution Reconsidered," *Political Science Quarterly* 34 (1919): 61–78.

Scots Magazine
>   *The Scots Magazine.* (Monthly magazine, Edinburgh).

[Sewall,] *Americans Roused*
[Jonathan Sewall,] *The Americans Roused, in a Cure for the Spleen*. New York, [1775].

Shalhope, *Roots of Democracy*
Robert E. Shalhope, *The Roots of Democracy: American Thought and Culture, 1760–1800*. Boston, 1990.

Sisson, "Idea of Revolution"
Daniel Sisson, "The Idea of Revolution in the Declaration of Independence and the Constitution," in *Constitutional Government in America: Essays and Proceedings from Southwestern University Law Review's First West Coast Conference on Constitutional Law*. Edited by Ronald K. L. Collins. Durham, N.C., 1980.

Smith, "David Ramsay"
Page Smith, "David Ramsay and the American Revolution," *William and Mary Quarterly* 17 (1960): 51–77.

South-Carolina Gazette
(Weekly newspaper, Charles Town, S.C.)

Southwick, "Molasses Act"
Albert B. Southwick, "The Molassess Act—Source of Precedents," *William and Mary Quarterly* 8 (1951): 389–405.

Thacher, *Sentiments*
Oxenbridge Thacher, *The Sentiments of a British American* (1764), reprinted in Bailyn *Pamphlets*, pp. 490–98.

They Preached Liberty
They Preached Liberty: With an Introductory Essay and Biographical Sketches by Franklin P. Cole. Indianapolis, [1977].

Town and Country Magazine
The Town and Country Magazine; or Universal Repository of Knowledge, Instruction, and Entertainment. (Monthly magazine, London.)

Trumbull Papers
The Trumbull Papers. Collections of the Massachusetts Historical Society. 5th Series, vol. 9. Boston, 1885.

Tucker and Hendrickson, *Fall*
Robert W. Tucker and David C. Hendrickson, *The Fall of the First British Empire: Origins of the War of American Independence*. Baltimore, 1982.

Waters, *Ipswich in the Massachusetts Bay Colony*
Thomas Franklin Waters, *Ipswich in the Massachusetts Bay Colony. Volume II. A History of the Town from 1700 to 1917*. Ipswich, Mass., 1917.

[Wells,] *Political Reflections*
[Richard Wells,] *A Few Political Reflections Submitted to the Consideration of the British Colonies, by a Citizen of Philadelphia*. Philadelphia, 1774.

Wheeler, "Calvin's Case"
    Harvey Wheeler, "Calvin's Case (1608) and the McIlwain-Schuyler Debate,"
    American Historical Review 61 (1956): 587–97.

Wickwire, *Subministers*
    Franklin B. Wickwire, *British Subministers and Colonial America 1763–1783.*
    Princeton, N.J., 1966.

Williams, "Book Review"
    David C. Williams, "Book Review," *William & Mary Quarterly* 50 (1993): 191–
    94 (reviewing Richard C. Sinopoli, *The Foundations of American Citizenship:
    Liberalism, the Constitution, and Civic Virtue.* New York, 1992).

Wood, *Creation*
    Gordon S. Wood, *The Creation of the American Republic 1776–1787.* Chapel
    Hill, N.C., 1969.

Wood, *Radicalism of American Revolution*
    Gordon S. Wood, *The Radicalism of the American Revolution.* New York,
    1992.

Wood, "Rhetoric and Reality"
    Gordon S. Wood, "Rhetoric and Reality in the American Revolution," in *In
    Search of Early America: The William & Mary Quarterly, 1943–1993.* Wil-
    liamsburg, Va., 1993, pp. 54–77.

[Wood,] *Institute of the Law*
    [Thomas Wood,] *A New Institute of the Imperial or Civil Law. With Notes,
    Shewing in some Principal Cases, amongst other Observations, How the
    Canon Law, the Laws of England, and the Laws and Customs of other Nations
    differ from it. In Four Books.* London, 1704.

Wright, *Fabric of Freedom*
    Esmond Wright, *Fabric of Freedom, 1763–1800.* New York, 1961.

NOTES

Historiographical Preface

1 [Wells,] *Political Reflections,* p. 3.
2 See, e.g., Smith, "David Ramsay."
3 See, e.g., Bancroft, *History.*
4 Fisher, *True History,* p. 9.
5 See *post,* pp. 97–99.
6 Becker, *History of Political Parties.*
7 Schlesinger, "American Revolution."
8 Smith, "David Ramsay," p. 70.
9 See, e.g., Brown, "Economic Democracy."
10 See, e.g., Brown, "Democracy."
11 Brown, "Revolution as Conservative Movement," p. 72.
12 Bailyn, "Revolution and Enlightenment," p. 93.
13 Main, *Social Structure,* pp. 68, 163.
14 Billias, "Introduction," p. 6.
15 Colbourn, *Lamp of Experience,* p. 191.
16 Rossiter, "Shaping American Tradition," p. 533.
17 Appleby, "Different Independence," p. 261.
18 Greene, "Changing Interpretations," p. 172.
19 ***Authority to Legislate, pp. 17–33.***
20 Wood, "Rhetoric and Reality," p. 69.

21 *Authority to Legislate, pp. 79, 120–21; Authority of Law, pp. 156–59.*
22 Wood, "Rhetoric and Reality," p. 71.
23 Bailyn, *Pamphlets*, p. 26.
24 Wood, "Rhetoric and Reality," pp. 71, 62.
25 Blackstone, *Commentaries* 3:254–55.
26 Bailyn, *Pamphlets*, p. 294.
27 Bloch, "Constitution and Culture," p. 551.
28 Appleby, "Different Independence," p. 262.
29 Williams, "Book Review," p. 192.
30 Shalhope, *Roots of Democracy*, p. 40.
31 Kerber, "Revolutionary Generation," p. 29.
32 Cornell, "Early American History," p. 341.
33 See generally, Greene, *Peripheries and Center*.
34 See *post*, p. 77–78.
35 Morgan, "American Revolution," p. 51.
36 *Authority of Law, pp. 156–57.*
37 Smith, "David Ramsay," p. 72.

JURISPRUDENTIAL PREFACE

1 Protest of the Lords, 11 May 1774, *Proceedings and Debates* 4:419.
2 Wood, *Creation*, p. 11 *(Authority to Tax, pp. 3–4)*.
3 *Authority to Tax, pp. 3–4.*
4 Bell v. Burlington, 34 *Ontario* 619, 622 (1915) (per Riddell, J.).
5 [Butler,] *Standing Army*, p. 27; Anon., *Budget Inscribed*, p. 4n *(Authority to Tax, p. 5)*.
6 Speech of Edmund Burke, Commons Debates, 31 January 1770, *Burke Writings* 2:235.
7 For example, see *In a Defiant Stance*; *In a Rebellious Spirit*; *In Defiance of the Law*; "In a Defensive Rage."

CHAPTER ONE: THE AUTHORITY OF THE CONSTITUTION

1 Handlin, *Popular Sources*, p. 153; *They Preached Liberty*, p. 171 *(Authority of Rights, pp. 5–6)*.
2 *Political Register* 7 (1770): 152; [Hartley,] *Appeal to Juries*, p. 4 *(Authority of Rights, p. 6)*.
3 Aldridge, "Paine and Dickinson," p. 135 *(Authority of Rights, p. 6)*.
4 For an extensive discussion of these rights, see *Authority of Rights, passim*.
5 *In Defiance of the Law*, pp. 32–49.
6 "Jurisprudence of Liberty," pp. 147–231.
7 Hale, "Reflections," p. 507; [Burnet,] *Submission to Supream Authority*, p. 3; Davis, *Reports*, "Preface," p. 3 *(Authority to Tax, p. 184)*.
8 [Wood,] *Institute of the Laws*, pp. 9–10; Anon., *Examination of the Legality*, pp. 4–5 *(Authority to Tax, p. 185)*.

9 Jenkins, *Works*, p. 34; "L.," *Letter to G[renville]*, pp. 35–36 *(Authority to Tax, pp. 185–86)*.

10 Anon., *Arguments to Prove*, pp. 7–8 *(Authority to Legislate, p. 153)*.

11 Pocock, *Politics*, p. 226 *(Authority to Legislate, pp. 153–54)*.

12 *New London Gazette*, 20 September 1765, reprinted in *Boston Evening-Post*, 14 October 1765, p. 1, col. 2 *(Authority of Rights, p. 97)*.

13 Jenkins, *Works of Judge Jenkins*, p. 128; *Gentleman's Magazine* 35 (1765): 558 [*sic*] 570; Anon., *Licentiousness Unmask'd*, p. 27 *(Authority of Rights, p. 98)*.

14 Speech of Sir George Moore, Commons Debates, 15 December 1621, [Nicholas,] *Proceedings of 1620–21*, 2: 330; Hawles, *Englishman's Right*, pp. 28, 39 *(Authority of Rights, p. 98)*.

15 Speech of the Lord Mayor, 12 April 1770, *Political Register* 6 (1770): 303 *(Authority of Rights, pp. 99–100)*.

16 Lucas, *Divelina Libera*, p. 5; Speech of Sir Edward Coke, 3 April 1628, *Conference of Both Houses*, p. 69; Howard, *Road from Runnymede*, p. 89 (quoting Penn) *(Authority of Rights, p. 100)*.

17 Protestation of 5 June 1628, *Commons Debates 1628*, 4:133 *(Authority of Rights, p. 100)*. Similarly, see *Concept of Liberty*, pp. 23–25.

18 [Fitch et al.,] *Reasons Why*, p. 26 *(Authority of Rights, pp. 66–67)*.

19 Anon., *Fair Trial*, p. 75; Johnson, *Notes on Pastoral*, p. 61; Anon., *Observations upon the Authority*, p. 33; Anon., *Conduct of Mansfield*, pp. 4–5 *(Authority of Rights, p. 67)*.

20 Cohen, "Revolution and Natural Law," pp. 498–99 (quoting John Adams); "To the Inhabitants of Salem," 11 July 1768, *Scots Magazine* 30 (1768): 523 *(Authority of Rights, p. 128)*.

21 Brown, *Revolutionary Politics*, p. 116; Mayhew, *Snare Broken*, p. 16; Chauncy, *Civil Magistrates*, p. 33; Baldwin, *New England Clergy*, p. 108; [Johnson,] *Important Observations*, p. 35 *(Authority of Rights, pp. 128–29)*.

22 Petition of 24 June 1769, *Addresses and Petitions of Common Council*, p. 6; East India Petition to House of Commons, 14 December 1772, *Scots Magazine* 35 (1773): 122; Speech of the Earl of Chatham, Lords Debates, 26 May 1774, *American Archives* (4th. ser.) 1:167; Petition of Lord Mayor et al., to House of Commons, 28 May 1773, *London Magazine* 43 (1774): 417 *(Authority of Rights, p. 67)*.

23 [Mulgrave,] *Letter from a Member*, p. 21; [Forster,] *Answer to the Question Stated*, p. 34; [Heath,] *Case of Devon Excise*, p. 31 (see also p. 3); Wickwire, *Subministers*, p. 191 (quoting Yorke) *(Authority to Legislate, pp. 159–60)*.

24 Replication of the Governor, 16 February 1773, *Briefs of Revolution*, p. 99 *(Authority to Legislate, p. 160)*.

25 Keir, *Constitutional History*, p. 363 *(Authority to Legislate, p. 161)*.

26 American whigs denied that these acknowledgments were precedents supporting Parliament's authority on various grounds: 1) that these statutes had not claimed supremacy; 2) were often adopted by American assemblies and thus binding on a colony due to American, not parliamentary authority; or 3) dealt with areas of constitutional competency that colonial whigs acknowledged was within the purview of Parliament.

27 "Irrelevance of the Declaration," p. 48.
28 For a preliminary list of ten reasons why it has been mistakenly accorded such
   prominence, see "Irrelevance of the Declaration," pp. 49–69.
29 "Irrelevance of the Declaration," pp. 50–51.
30 "Irrelevance of the Declaration," pp. 68–69.
31 "In our Contracted Sphere," p. 21.
32 See Wood, *Radicalism of American Revolution*, p. 166.
33 "In our Contracted Sphere," pp. 22–24.
34 "In our Contracted Sphere," pp. 24–25.
35 Hopkins, *Rights*, p. 510; *Gentleman's Magazine* 35 (1765): 561 *(Authority to Tax,
   pp. 57–58)*.
36 "In our Contracted Sphere," p. 26.
37 Anon., *Policy of the Laws*, pp. 24–31; [Rawson,] *Revolution in New England*,
   p. 43 *(Authority of Rights, pp. 140–41)*.
38 For the eighteenth-century dichotomy between "right" and "power" in jurisprudential theory, see "In the Taught Tradition," pp. 947–61.
39 "Rule of Law," p. 629.
40 "Rule of Law," pp. 629–30.
41 "Rule of Law," p. 630.
42 "Rule of Law," pp. 630–31.
43 "Rule of Law," p. 631.
44 "Rule of Law," p. 631.

CHAPTER TWO: THE AUTHORITY TO TAX

1 Raising a political (not a constitutional) defense, Americans contended the troops
   were maintained for British purposes, not colonial. *In Defiance of the Law*,
   pp. 63–79.
2 *Authority of Rights, pp. 11–15; Concept of Liberty*, pp. 13–19.
3 *Authority to Tax, pp. 44–52; Authority to Legislate, pp. 207–45.*
4 For the relevance and meaning of legal time in the American colonial context,
   see *Authority to Tax, pp. 186–89.*
5 *Authority to Tax, pp. 158–66.*
6 *Authority to Tax, p. 48.*
7 Unlike "legislation," tax bills had to originate in the House of Commons and
   could only be approved or rejected by the Lords, not amended.
8 *Authority to Tax, pp. 85–96.*
9 *Authority to Tax, pp. 158–70.*
10 *Authority to Tax, pp. 170–71.*
11 Testimony of Benjamin Franklin, House of Commons, 13 February 1766, Ryder,
   "Parliamentary Diaries," p. 301; Boston Committee of Correspondence quoted
   in Brown, *Revolutionary Politics*, p. 181; Boston Committee of Correspondence to the Committees of Salem, Marblehead, Newburyport, and Portsmouth, 24 March 1774, in Brown, *Revolutionary Politics*, p. 183 *(Authority to
   Tax, pp. 174–77)*.
12 Brown, *Revolutionary Politics*, p. 184; "Extract of a Letter from a Gentleman at

New-York to his Friend in this Town, dated Feb. 28, 1774," *Gazette & Post-Boy*, 21 March 1774, p. 3, col. 1; *Boston Evening Post*, 21 March 1774, p. 2, col. 3 *(Authority to Tax, pp. 177–78)*.

13 *Authority to Legislate, pp. 9–10, 294–98, 306–8.*

14 *Boston Post-Boy*, 27 January 1766, p. 2, col. 3; Address from a Committee of Gentlemen to Governor William Tryon, November 1765, ibid., p. 2, col. 3; from the *North Carolina Gazette*, 20 November, 1765, *North Carolina Colonial Records*, 7:129 *(Authority to Tax, pp. 132–33)*.

15 "In a Defensive Rage," pp. 1043–91; *In a Defiant Stance*, pp. 168–73.

16 *Authority to Tax, pp. 29–31.*

17 Historians of the "progressive" era, misreading the evidence, concluded that Americans objected that the Stamp Act was unconstitutional because it was an "internal" tax. As a result, a distinction between "internal" and "external" taxes has been emphasized in the historical literature. It played no role, however, in the revolutionary debate and need not be discussed in this book. For discussion, see *Authority to Tax, pp. 33–39.*

18 *In a Rebellious Spirit*, pp. 48–99; *In a Defiant Stance*, pp. 118–24; "In a Defensive Rage."

19 *Authority to Tax, pp. 31, 226–31, 264–70.*

20 *Authority to Tax, pp. 12–14, 16–21.*

21 *Boston News-Letter*, 10 May 1764, p. 2, col. 3 *(Authority to Tax, p. 12)*.

22 Lee, *Election Sermon*, p. 14; Hopkins, *Rights*, pp. 510, 507; *Gentleman's Magazine* 4 (1774): 310 *(Authority to Tax, p. 54)*.

23 Letter from the Massachusetts House of Representatives to Agent Dennys de Berdt, 12 January 1768, Adams, *Writings*, 1:139–40; Petition from the Council and House of Burgesses of Virginia to the King, 18 December 1764, *Journal of Burgesses* 10:302 *(Authority to Tax, p. 60)*.

24 Petition from the Council and House of Burgesses of Virginia to the King, 18 December 1764, *Journal of Burgesses* 10:302 *(Authority to Tax, p. 60)*.

25 Instruction to the Town of Ipswich, 21 October 1765, in Waters, *Ipswich in Massachusetts Bay Colony*, 2:294; Resolves of Fairfax County, 18 July 1774, *Revolutionary Virginia*, 1:127 *(Authority to Tax, p. 61)*.

26 For extended discussion of the settlement contract and the settlement debt, see *Authority to Tax, pp. 60–64.*

27 Instructions of the House of Representatives to Richard Jackson, 22 September 1764, *Pennsylvania Archives* 7:5643–44 *(Authority to Tax, pp. 63–64)*.

28 [Goodricke,] *Observations on Price's Theory*, p. 31; Speech of George Grenville, Commons Debates, 14 January 1766, Anon., *Celebrated Speech*, p. 10 *(Authority to Tax, p. 66)*.

29 McAdam, *Johnson and Law*, p. 105 *(Authority to Tax, p. 67)*.

30 Anon., *To the People of Britain in General*, p. 54; *Critical Review*, 22 (1766): 349; Anon., *To the People of Britan in General*, p. 26 *(Authority to Tax, p. 67)*.

31 Thacher, *Sentiments*, p. 492; Anon., *Case of Great Britain*, pp. 10–11 *(Authority to Tax, p. 70)*.

32 *Authority to Tax, pp. 71–73.* For the extensive debate over who benefitted from the war, see 73–74.

33 Anon., *Constitutional Answer to Wesley*, p. 18; Hartley, *Speech and Motions*, p. 11 *(Authority to Tax, p. 75)*.

34 Letter from the Virginia House of Burgesses to the Pennsylvania House of Representatives, 9 May 1768, *Pennsylvania Archives* 7:6191; South Carolina Resolves, 29 November 1765, Morgan, *Prologue*, p. 58; [Mitchell,] *The Present State*, p. 319 *(Authority to Tax, p. 78)*.

35 Pitt's Speech on Repeal of the Stamp Act, in Morgan, *Prologue*, p. 140 *(Authority to Tax, p. 78)*.

36 Speech of the Duke of Grafton, Lords Debates, 11 March 1766, "Stamp Act Debates," p. 581; Burgh, *Political Disquisitions*, 2:275, 280 *(Authority to Tax, p. 79)*.

37 Instructions of Providence, 13 August 1765, *Boston Post-Boy*, 19 August 1765, p. 3, cols. 1–2; *Boston Evening-Post*, 19 August 1765, p. 2, col. 3; Rhode Island Resolves, September 1765, in Morgan, *Prologue*, pp. 50–51 *(Authority to Tax, p. 181)*.

38 *Journal of the Times*, 24 October 1768, p. 10, col. 2; Instructions of Providence, 13 August 1765, *Boston Post-Boy*, 19 August 1765, p. 3, cols. 1–2; *Boston Evening-Post*, 19 August 1765, p. 2, col. 3; Rhode Island Resolves, September 1765, in Morgan, *Prologue*, pp. 50–51 *(Authority to Tax, p. 181)*. Remember, liberty was property that the eighteenth-century British owned by custom. *Concept of Liberty*, pp. 22–25.

39 "In Accordance with Usage," pp. 335–68 *(Authority to Tax, pp. 181–93)*.

40 *Reasons Why the British Colonies . . . Should not be Charged with Internal Taxes* (1764), reprinted in Bailyn, *Pamphlets*, pp. 391–92.

41 *Authority of Rights, pp. 34–38* (right to security), pp. 39–46 (right to government).

42 *Authority of Rights, pp. 27–33.*

43 This was the American perspective. It was by no means as clear as they thought that, in the matter of jury trials, the Stamp Act treated them differently than their fellow subjects in Britain were treated. *Authority of Rights, pp. 47–59.*

44 E.g., see *Authority of Rights, pp. 27–59.*

45 Pennsylvania Resolves, 21 September 1765, *Prior Documents*, p. 21 *(Authority to Tax, p. 108)*.

46 *Authority to Tax, pp. 111–15.*

47 For their arguments, see *Authority to Tax, pp. 118–21.*

48 [Ramsay,] *Historical Essay*, p. 196; Remonstrance and Petition of the Lord Mayor, Aldermen, and Livery of London to the King, 11 April 1775, *London Magazine* 44 (1775): 209 *(Authority to Tax, pp. 115–16)*.

49 For discussion, see *Authority to Tax, pp. 141–46.*

50 Care, *English Liberties Boston Edition*, p. 58–62; Pym, *Proceedings against Manwaring*, p. 10 *(Authority to Tax, p. 136)*.

51 The *New London Gazette* quoted in *Boston Evening-Post*, 28 October 1765, p. 1, col. 2; Anon., *Prospect of Consequences*, p. 16; Anon., *Letter to Cooper*, p. 32 *(Authority to Tax, pp. 139–40)*.

52 Marvell, *Account*, p. 4 *(Authority to Tax, pp. 140–41)*.

53 Speech of George Grenville, Commons Debates, 14 January 1766, *Parliamentary*

History, 16:101; Morgan, *Prologue,* p. 137; Speech of William Pitt, Commons Debates, 14 January 1766, *Parliamentary History,* 16:104; Anon., *Celebrated Speech,* pp. 12–13; Morgan, *Prologue,* p. 139 *(Authority to Tax, p. 152).*

54 Anon., *To Tax Themselves,* p. 119 *(Authority to Tax, pp. 152–53).*

55 *Demophoon,* "A Dissertation on the Original Dispute between Great-Britain and her Colonies," *Political Register* 7 (1770): 155; *London Magazine* 39 (1770): 418 *(Authority to Tax, p. 154).*

56 For discussion, see *Authority to Tax, pp. 154–57.*

57 *Concept of Representation,* pp. 50–51.

58 *Concept of Representation,* pp. 51–52.

59 *Concept of Representation,* pp. 52–53.

60 Fox, *Speech of 2 July,* pp. 23–24 *(Authority of Law, p. 86).*

61 James Wilson, "Parliamentary Authority," 17 August 1774, reprinted in *Commemoration Ceremony,* p. 57 *(Authority of Law, p. 87).*

62 Price, *Two Tracts: Tract One,* p. 48; James Wilson, "Parliamentary Authority," 17 August 1774, reprinted in *Commemoration Ceremony,* p. 57; "A Freeholder in the county of Worcester," *Gazette & News-Letter,* 9 March 1775, p. 2, col. 1 *(Authority of Law, p. 87).*

63 *Concept of Representation,* p. 61.

CHAPTER THREE: THE AUTHORITY TO LEGISLATE

1 Hardwicke's Reports, 11 March 1766, *Proceedings and Debates* 2:342 (reporting Speech of Lord Mansfield, Lords Debates, 11 March 1766); 6 George III, cap. 12; Speech of Charles Yorke, Common Debates, 3 February 1766, "Declaratory Debates," pp. 566–67 *(Authority to Legislate, pp. 46, 37, 38).*

2 Speech of Thomas Pownall, Commons Debates, 8 February 1769, *Proceedings and Debates,* 3:110 *(Authority to Legislate, p. 54).*

3 *Authority to Legislate, pp. 53–54, 52.*

4 *Authority to Legislate, pp. 87–89.*

5 Abingdon, *Thoughts on Burke's Letter,* pp. 12–13, xxxv *(Authority to Legislate, pp. 81–82).*

6 Kemp, "Parliamentary Sovereignty," p. 12 (quoting Abingdon); [Mulgrave,] *Letter From a Member,* p. 7; McAdam, *Johnson and Law,* p. 189 (quoting Johnson); "Junius," *Junius* 1:v–vi *(Authority to Legislate, pp. 82–83).*

7 *St. Patrick's Anti-Stamp Chronicle* 2 (1774): 54 *(Authority to Legislate, p. 90).*

8 Trenchard, Letter of 8 June 1723, *Cato's Letters* 4:231; Lockwood, *Connecticut Election Sermon,* p. 7; Fiske, *Importance of Righteousness,* p. 31 *(Authority to Legislate, pp. 97–98).*

9 *Authority to Legislate, pp. 100–107.*

10 Speech of Lord Lyttleton, Lords Debates, 3 February 1766, *Proceedings and Debates,* 2:126; Anon., *Serious and Impartial Observations,* p. 34 *(Authority to Legislate, 112–13).*

11 "Humble Representation of the Lords Spiritual and Temporal," 17 October 1719, *Protest of Lords of Ireland,* pp. 40–41 *(Authority to Legislate, p. 115).*

12 "Some Thoughts on the Constitution," Philadelphia, 12 June 1775, *American*

Archives 2:963; Resolves of Pembroke, 28 December 1772, *Boston Evening-Post*, 11 January 1773, p. 2, col. 2 *(Authority to Legislate, pp. 115–16)*.

13 Hoadly, *Works*, 2:256; "Some Thoughts on the Constitution," Philadelphia, 12 June 1775, *American Archives* 2: 962; [Hawley,] "To the Inhabitants," 13 April 1775, *American Archives* 2:334 *(Authority to Legislate, pp. 118–19)*.

14 Paley, *Principles of Philosophy*, pp. 417–18 *(Authority to Legislate, p. 120)*.

15 Pocock, *Politics*, p. 226 (quoting a Commons speech Burke did not deliver) *(Authority to Legislate, p. 128)*.

16 Jones, *Constitutional Criterion*, p. 14 *(Authority to Legislate, pp. 128–29)*.

17 Speech of Sir William Meredith, Commons Debates, 10 December 1777, *Parliamentary History* 19:588; [Joseph Hawley,] "To the Inhabitants of the Massachusetts-Bay," 9 March 1775, *American Archives* 2:96–97 *(Authority to Legislate, pp. 142–43)*.

18 Anon., *Four Letters*, p. 19; Sisson, "Idea of Revolution," p. 411 *(Authority to Legislate, p. 146)*.

19 Anon., *Common Sense Conferences*, p. 7; [Ramsay,] *Historical Essay*, p. 115 *(Authority to Legislate, pp. 146–47)*.

20 Demophilus, *Genuine Principles*, p. 35 *(Authority to Legislate, p. 147)*.

21 Answer from the House of Representatives to Governor Francis Bernard, 24 October 1765, *Boston News-Letter*, 31 October 1765, p. 1, col. 2 *(Authority to Legislate, p. 148)*.

22 *Authority to Legislate, pp. 172–91.*

23 *Authority to Legislate, pp. 192–206.*

24 [Sewall,] *Americans Roused*, p. 12 *(Authority to Legislate, p. 161)*.

25 For a detailed example of the use of forensic history by two parties to the controversy debating constitutional doctrines by using what they treated as history, see *Briefs of Revolution*, pp. 103–12; *Authority to Legislate, pp. 159–71;* "Jurisprudence of Liberty," pp. 211–31.

26 Letter from the Continental Congress to the People of Great Britain, 5 September 1774, *London Magazine* 43 (1774): 629 *(Authority to Legislate, pp. 207–18)*.

27 Resolves of the South Carolina Convention, 8 July 1774, *American Archives* 1:526; Jack P. Greene, "Introduction" to *Commemoration Ceremony*, p. 41 *(Authority to Legislate, pp. 218–21)*.

28 24 George II, cap. 53 *(Authority to Legislate, pp. 262–63)*.

29 [Lind,] *Thirteenth Parliament*, p. 237 *(Authority to Legislate, p. 263)*.

30 Petition of Richard Partridge, Agent for Pennsylvania, to the House of Commons, 15 March 1748/49, *Proceedings and Debates of Parliaments* 5:306–7; Petition of Richard Partridge, Agent for Rhode Island, to the House of Commons, 1 April 1751, ibid., p. 474; Petition same to same, 15 March 1748/49, ibid., p. 307 *(Authority to Legislate, p. 263)*.

31 Declarations and Resolves, 14 October 1774, *Journals of Congress* 1:71–72; Petition of General Assembly to the King, 25 March 1775, *Journal of New York Assembly* (1766–76), p. 11 *(Authority to Legislate, pp. 265–66)*.

32 Anon., *Supremacy of Legislature*, p. 27; Lee, *Appeal to Justice*, pp. 26–27 *(Authority to Legislate, pp. 268–69)*.

33 *South-Carolina Gazette*, 27 July 1767, p. 1, col. 3 (reprinting *Benevolus*) *(Authority to Legislate, p. 270).*

34 *In Defiance of the Law*, pp. 6–7, 88–93; *In a Defiant Stance*, pp. 108–11.

35 Address from Commons House to Governor James Wright, 18 February 1767, *Georgia Commons House Journal* 14:441 *(Authority to Legislate, pp. 274–75).*

36 Address from the New York General Assembly to Governor Henry Moore, *Gentlemen's Magazine* 37 (1767): 89 *(Authority to Legislate, p. 275).*

37 7 George III, cap. 59; Letter from William Samuel Johnson to Governor William Pitkin, 16 May 1767, *Trumbull Papers*, p. 232; Dickinson, *Letters*, p. 310 *(Authority to Legislate, pp. 276–77).*

38 Letter from Governor Henry Moore to Lord Shelbourne, 21 August 1767, *New York Colonial Documents*, pp. 948–49 *(Authority to Legislate, pp. 277–78).*

39 Minutes for 12 August 1768, *Acts of the Privy Council*, p. 139; Letter from George Grenville to Thomas Whately, 13 April 1768, *Grenville Letterbooks (Authority to Legislate, pp. 278–79).*

40 *In a Rebellious Spirit*, pp. 86–126.

41 "An act for the trial of treasons comit[t]ed out of the King's dominions." 35 Henry VIII, cap. 2 *(Authority to Legislate, pp. 281–82).*

42 South Carolina Resolves, 19 August 1769, *Boston Chronicle*, p. 316, col. 1; Address from the House of Assembly, 17 June 1769, *Delaware House Minutes* (1765–70), p. 218; Address of the North Carolina House of Assembly to the King, October 1769, *Boston Evening-Post*, 22 January 1770, p. 4, col. 1 *(Authority to Legislate, pp. 281–86).*

43 Speech of Thomas Pownall, Commons Debates, 5 March 1770, *Proceedings and Debates* 3:218; Speech of Thomas Pownall, Commons Debates, 19 April 1769, ibid., p. 155 *(Authority to Legislate, p. 287).*

44 Letter from William Samuel Johnson to Governor William Pitkin, 26 April 1769, *Trumbull Papers*, pp. 336–37 *(Authority to Legislate, pp. 288–89).*

45 Letter from William Samuel Johnson to Governor William Pitkin, 20 October 1768, *Trumbull Papers*, p. 296; Letter from William Knox to George Grenville, 15 December 1768, *Grenville Papers* 4:400; Letter from William Samuel Johnson to Governor William Pitkin, 23 March 1769, *Trumbull Papers*, p. 324 *(Authority to Legislate, pp. 289–90).*

46 Speech of Lord North, Commons Debates, 5 March 1770, *Proceedings and Debates*, 3:213; Speech of Lord Rockingham, Lords Debates, 18 March 1774, *Proceedings and Debates*, 4:434; Petition of the House of Burgesses to the King, 27 June 1770, *Revolution Documents* 2:129 *(Authority to Legislate, pp. 291–92).*

47 Speech of Charles Wolfran Cornwall, Commons Debates, 19 April 1774, *Proceedings and Debates*, p. 236 *(Authority to Legislate, pp. 297–98).*

48 Speech of Thomas Townshend, Jr., Commons Debates, 19 April 1774, *Proceedings and Debates*, p. 236; Speech of John Burgoyne, Commons Debates, 19 April 1774, ibid., pp. 232, 229; Speech of Lord George Germain, Commons Debates, 2 May 1774, ibid., p. 381 *(Authority to Legislate, pp. 298–99).*

CHAPTER FOUR: THE AUTHORITY TO REGULATE

1 Instruction of the Pennsylvania Congress, 15 July 1774, *London Magazine* 43 (1774): 586–87 *(Authority to Legislate, p. 221)*.

2 *Boston Gazette*, 27 January 1772, reprinted in Adams, *Writings* 2:323; Southwick, "Molasses Act," p. 399 *(Authority to Legislate, pp. 222–23)*.

3 New York Petition to Commons, 18 October 1764, Morgan, *Prologue*, pp. 11–12; Representation and Remonstrance of New York General Assembly to the House of Commons, 25 March 1775, *Gentleman's Magazine* 45 (1775): 248; Petyt, *Lex Parliamentaria*, p. 32 *(Authority to Legislate, pp. 223–27)*.

4 Anon., *Considerations Upon Rights of Colonists*, p. 11; "James Duane's Propositions," 7–22 September 1774, *Letters of Delegates to Congress* 1:38 *(Authority to Legislate, p. 233)*.

5 For the several constitutional theories suggested—necessity, contract, custom, federalism, natural law—see *Authority to Legislate, pp. 227–37*.

6 John Adams, "Notes of Debates," 28 September 1774, *Letters of Delegates to Congress* 1:111; "James Duane's Propositions Before the Committee on Rights," 7–22 September 1774, ibid., pp. 39, 41 *(Authority to Legislate, p. 241)*.

7 "James Duane's Notes for a Speech in Congress," 13 October 1774, *Letters of Delegates to Congress*, pp. 189, 190; "John Adam's Diary," 13 October 1774, ibid., p. 189 *(Authority to Legislate, pp. 241–42)*.

8 Declaration of Rights, 14 October 1774, *Journal of the First Congress*, p. 61 *(Authority to Legislate, pp. 242–43)*.

9 General Conway's Bill for Conciliation with the Colonies, 5 May 1780, Conway, *Peace Speech*, p. 49; Representation and Remonstrance of New York General Assembly to the House of Commons, 25 March 1775, *Journal of New York Assembly* (1766–76), p. 116 *(Authority to Legislate, pp. 243–44)*.

10 Letter from the New York Committee of Correspondence to the Mayor, Alderman, and Common Council of London, 5 May 1775, *Scots Magazine* 37 (1775): 400; Address, Remonstrance, and Petition of the Lord Mayor, Alderman, and Livery of London to the King, 11 April 1775, *London Magazine* 44 (1775): 209 *(Authority to Legislate, p. 244)*.

11 Morgan, "Colonial Ideas," p. 341; Morgan, *Challenge*, pp. 3–4 *(Authority to Legislate, pp. 303–4)*.

12 Degler, "Preface 3," p. 41; Bailyn, *Ideological Origins*, p. 218 *(Authority to Legislate, p. 305)*.

13 Morgan, *Birth*, p. 51; Bailyn, *Pamphlets*, p. 384 *(Authority to Legislate, p. 305)*.

14 Resolution of 6 December 1769, *New Jersey Votes and Proceedings* (1769), p. 88; Resolves of 16 May 1769, *Journal of Burgesses* 11:214; Resolution of Maryland Lower House, 28 December 1769, *Boston Chronicle*, 18 January 1770, p. 22, col. 3 *(Authority to Legislate, p. 307)*.

CHAPTER FIVE: THE AUTHORITY OF THE PREROGATIVE

1 Speech of Lord North, Commons Debates, 26 April 1773, *Proceedings and Debates*, 3:488–89 *(Authority to Legislate, pp. 293–94)*.

2 Speeches of Charles Jenkinson and Lord North, Commons Debates, 26 April 1773, *Proceedings and Debates,* pp. 489, 490; Speeches of Charles Wolfran Cornwall, Commons Debates, 19 April 1774, ibid., 4:236, 230; Speech of Edmund Burke, 19 April 1774, Commons Debates, ibid., 4:230; Speech of Charles James Fox, Commons Debates, 19 April 1774, ibid., 4:238 *(Authority to Legislate, pp. 294–95).*

3 Letter from Governor Thomas Hutchinson to Sir Francis Bernard, 1 January 1774, quoted in Knollenberg, "Adams and the Tea Party," p. 497 *(Authority to Legislate, pp. 296–97).*

4 *Gazette and Post-Boy* (Supplement), 2 May 1774, p. 1, col. 2 (quoting London newspaper of 12 March 1774) *(Authority of Law, p. 9).*

5 14 George III, cap. 19; Speech of Lord North, Commons Debates, 14 March 1774, *Proceedings and Debates* 4:60; Speech of Lord North, Commons Debates, 25 March 1774, ibid., 4:143 *(Authority of Law, pp. 9–10).*

6 Speech of Lord North, Commons Debates, 23 March 1774, *Proceedings and Debates* 4:108–9 *(Authority of Law, p. 10).*

7 New York City Resolves, 19 July 1774, *Boston Evening-Post,* 1 August 1774, p. 2, col. 2; Resolves of Charles Town, South Carolina, July 1774, *American Archives* 1:316; "To All the English Colonies of North America," Philadelphia, 1 July 1774, ibid., 1:378; Letter from Richard Henry Lee to Arthur Lee, 26 June 1774, *Lee Letters,* p. 114 *(Authority of Law, pp. 10–11).*

8 Resolves of New Shoreham Town Meeting, 2 March 1774, *Rhode Island Colony Records* 7:277 *(Authority to Legislate, p. 309).*

9 Tucker & Hendrickson, *Fall,* p. 179 *(Authority of Law, p. 151).*

10 Petition of Virginia Council and House to the King, 18 December 1764, *Journal of Burgesses* 10:302; *Gazette and News-Letter,* 21 March 1765, p. 2, col. 1; Petition to the King, 26 October 1774, *Journals of Congress,* 1:119, 120 *(Authority of Law, pp. 152–53).*

11 Resolves of Granville County, North Carolina, Rakove, *Beginnings,* p. 32; "To the Inhabitants of New-York," 6 October, 1774, *American Archives* 1:826 *(Authority of Law, p. 153).*

12 Address, Remonstrance and Petition of the Lord Mayor, *et al.* to the King and the Answer of the King to the Address, 23 March 1770, *Town and Country Magazine* 7 (1770): 128. For a more extended discussion of the constitutional arguments of British "radicals," see *Authority of Law, pp. 160–61.*

13 Speech of Sir William DeGrey, Commons Debates, 25 January 1770, *Parliamentary History* 16:796–97 *(Authority of Law, p. 163).*

14 Speeches of Charles James Fox and Lord North, Commons Debates, 26 October 1775, *Proceedings and Debates* 6: 118–19 *(Authority of Law, p. 164).*

15 Speech of John Dunning, Commons Debates, 16 April 1780, *Parliamentary History* 21:347; *Boston Evening-Post,* 26 July 1773, p. 1, col. 3; Anon., *Some Reasons for Approving Gloucester's Plan,* p. 27 *(Authority of Law, pp. 164–65).*

16 Letter from Thomas Northcote to Irish Committee, 15 October 1783, *Collection of Irish Letters,* p. 95; Letter from William Samuel Johnson to Governor William Pitkin, 20 October 1768, *Trumbull Papers,* p. 296 *(Authority of Law, p. 166).*

17 Pemberton, *Lord North*, p. 236 *(Authority of Law, p. 166)*.
18 McIlwain, *Revolution*, p. 118 *(Authority of Law, pp. 166–67)*.
19 McIlwain, *Revolution*, pp. 118–19 *(Authority of Law, p. 167)*.
20 Greene, "Origins," p. 52 *(Authority of Law, pp. 167–68)*.
21 Wright, *Fabric of Freedom*, p. 81 *(Authority of Law, pp. 171–72)*.

CHAPTER 6: CONCLUSION

 1 *Authority to Legislate, pp. 228–30.*
 2 As with the other constitutional provisions cited in this chapter, the words of the
    Virginia Constitution were not selected because they are unique to Virginia or
    because Virginia first enunciated them. The examples are cited at random,
    with the purpose of showing that all the state constitutions were involved in
    the process of constitutional continuity. If selection were limited to those
    constitutions that pioneered provisions, most quotations would come from the
    New York and Massachusetts Constitutions.
 3 It should also be noted that the new American constitutions were influenced by
    constitutional controversies that occurred in Great Britain involving questions
    of constitutional law that were *not* in dispute between American whigs and
    London. For example, the provisions in the United States Constitution that
    members of the House of Representatives stand for election every two years
    (Article I, Section 2) owed something to the debate in Great Britain over
    frequent elections. The provision that "Each House shall be the Judge of the
    Elections . . . of its own Members" (Article I, Section 5) owed much to the
    dispute over the expulsion of John Wilkes from the House of Commons. In
    addition, the constitutional provisions against government search and seizure
    without a judicial warrant were influenced in large part by events that hap-
    pened in London during the 1760s and 1770s. In the colonies, British authori-
    ties had forced their way into no American houses or warehouses so there
    were no memories of "unconstitutional" searches in America before indepen-
    dence.
 4 *Authority to Legislate, pp. 128–34.*
 5 Article I, Section 10, *Constitution of the United States.*
 6 Article III, Section 2, *Constitution of the United States.*
 7 Article III, Section 2, *Constitution of the United States.*
 8 Article XXX, "Declaration of the Rights," *Constitution of Massachusetts* (1780).
 9 Article XII, "Declaration of the Rights," *Constitution of Massachusetts* (1780).
10 Section 39, *Magna Carta.*
11 Speech of Lord North, Commons Debates, 7 December 1768, *Proceedings and
    Debates* 3:32; Speech of George Johnstone, Commons Debates, ibid., 5:374
    (Authority to Legislate, p. 301).
12 For a discussion of the various proposals for resolving the predicament, see
    "Another Origin of Judicial Review," pp. 963–89.

INDEX

Abingdon, Willoughby Bertie, 4th earl of, 51
Act of 7 George III. *See* New York General
Assembly Suspending Act
Act of 14 George III. *See* Boston Port Act
Act of 35 Henry VIII, 66, 69–70, 82–83, 90,
104
Act to Punish Governors of Plantations . . .
for Crimes, 62
Act to regulate and restrain Paper Bills of
Credit, 63–65
Adams, John, xiv, 10, 76, 77, 97–98
Adams, Samuel, 74
American original contract. *See* Contract:
colonial original
American Revolution, causes of: "conspir-
acy" theory, xiii, xiv: constitutional and
ideological, ix–x, xi–xv, xix–xx, 57; eco-
nomic, xi, xv; modern historians' misun-
derstanding of, x–xvi; and republicanism,
xvi; trade regulation as, 74
American whigs, constitutional case of, in re
Parliament's authority to legislate for colonies: appeal to ancient and 17th-century

English constitutions, 13–14; appeal to
natural law, 13, 14–15; and authority of
contract, 15–20, 33–34; modern historians' misunderstanding of, 79–82, 84;
and regulation/legislation distinction, 101.
See also Avoidance strategy, constitutional
Analogy, as authority for constitutionalism, xix, 84; and doctrine of consent to
taxation, 41, 43–45; and Palatinate counties, 43–44; and Parliament's authority to
legislate for colonies, 59–60; precedents
of, 59–60, 84
Andrews, Charles M. (historian), x
Andros, Edmund, 19
Appleby, Joyce (historian), xii
Arbuthnot, John, 24
Arms: right to keep and bear in U.S. federal, state, and Glorious Revolution constitutions, 102
Attainder, bills of: prohibited in U.S. federal, state, and Glorious Revolution constitutions, 102
Austin, John, 97–98

Hawles, Sir John, 9
Hawley, Joseph, 55, 57
Heath, B., 12 and 131n.23
Henry I, king of England: coronation charter of, 17
Hillsborough, Wills Hill, 1st earl of, 71, 84, 96–97
History, forensic: inferences from, and precedent for parliamentary supremacy, 59, 60, 101, 136n.25
Hoadly, Benjamin, 55
Hopkins, Stephen, 18 and 132n.35, 33
Hume, David, 53
Hutchinson, Thomas, 13, 87–88

Impeachment, power of: in U.S. federal, state, and 17th-century English constitutions, 102
Indians, American: British trade with, 37
Influence: crown exercise of, and corruption, 20, 96, 98, 99
Innovation: effect of precedent on, 12
Intolerable acts. See Coercive acts
Ireland: analogy of to American colonies in re relationship to Parliament and crown, x, 44–45, 59–60, 75, 83, 96, 98; sources of rights claimed by, 9, 10, 19
Iron Act, 65–66

James II, king of England: and violation of the original contract, 17
Jefferson, Thomas, xiv
Jenkins, David, 6 and 131n.9, 8
Jenkinson, Charles, 86 and 139n.2
Jersey, Isle of. See Channel islands
Johnson, Dr. Samuel, 10 and 131n.19, 11 and 131n.21, 36, 51
Johnson, William Samuel, 68 and 137n.37, 70–71 and 137nn.44, 45, 96
Johnstone, George, 106 and 140n.11
Jones, William, 56
Judicial review, doctrine of: vs. legislative command, 105–6 and 140n.12
Judiciary: role of, in U.S. vs. Britain, 103, 106; tenure and salaries of, 102–3
Junius, 51

Keir, Sir David Lindsay (historian), 13–14
King. See Crown
Knox, William, 28, 38, 71, 137n.45

Law: as command vs. rule of law, 5; relationship of, to custom, 6, 7–8; role of, and 17th-century English vs. 18th-century British constitutions, x, xix, 3; role of, in U.S. federal and state constitutions, 102, 103, 105n. *See also* Constitutionalism, 18th-century vocabulary of: "law/legal"
—fundamental: limits of, on legislative authority, 52
—natural. *See* Natural law
—rule of: American whig appeal to, xv, 23, 25, as authority for constitutionalism, 20–25; as protector of rights, 22–23; relationship of, to liberty, 5, 21, 22, 57, 95; role of, in U.S. federal and state constitutions, 104–5, 106; vs. parliamentary supremacy and legislative command, x, 5, 21, 24, 52, 56, 57–59, 84; vs. royal prerogative, 5, 21, 22, 24, 57–58, 94, 104. *See also* Constitutionalism, 18th-century vocabulary of: "rule of law"
—statutory: and alteration of colonial legislation by parliamentary statute, 62–63
Lee, Arthur, 66
Lee, Jonathan, 33
Lee, Richard Henry, 89 and 139n.7
Leeds, England: as nonelector borough, and virtual representation, 46
Legislation, precedents of, for parliamentary supremacy over colonies, 59–72 *passim;* and colonial avoidance strategy, 67–69; and internal/external regulatory/revenue distinctions, 81; internal legislation as, 62, 63, 65–66; repeal of, as "surreptitious" precedent, 71; and 17th-century English, vs. 18th-century British constitutions, 62; vs. laws of general superintendence, 62–63
Legislation of supremacy: Parliament's utilization of, for supremacy over colonies, 66–71
Legislative supremacy: 17th-century English, vs. 18th-century British concepts of, x, 57, 62, 84
Legislators: immunity of, from arrest in U.S. federal, state, and Glorious Revolution constitutions, 102
Legislatures, colonial: and constitutional authority of custom, 6–7, 39–40; on Parliament's authority to regulate colonial trade, 61, 73–74, 74–75; and relationship of colonies to crown, 91–92